# First Grade Phonics & Reading

## Language & Reading Workbook

Visit **McRuffy.com** for helpful resources to teach this curriculum!

**Language & Reading Workbook (LAR)**
ISBN 978159269-1937

**McRuffy Press First Grade Phonics & Reading Curriculum**
ISBN 978159269-1968

Written and illustrated by
Brian Davis M. A. Ed.

Graphic Design by
Sherylynn Davis

McRuffy Press, LLC
P.O. Box 212
Raymore, MO 64083

816-331-7831

sales@mcruffy.com

**www.McRuffy.com**

# Jungle Reader Game

*Play games on the back of the worbook!*

**All games:** Use the reading book for the week to create questions for the games. Players answer a question or complete a task before earning a roll. Players will get a point for each correct answer or completed task. If a player lands on an elephant space, the player gets an extra point. When one player has reached the end (the X spot), the game ends and points are counted. Players may keep track of points using small objects such as counters, beans, or coins. Points can also be kept on paper as a scorecard. The player with the most points wins.

Use a die, spinner, or draw numbers to move on the board with game pieces (small objects or game pawns).

**Games** (tasks to complete before moving)

**Word List Reading Game:** Read a word from the list. You may limit it to words that are also a part of the week's phonics theme.

**Word List Meaning Game:** This game would most likely require an adult to create questions or clues. Direct questions to a player on their turn to find a word on the word list according to the meaning. It does not need to be a formal clue. Find a word that means ___. or What is something that ___?

**Word List Rhyme Game:** Find a word on the list that rhymes with ____.

**Word List Sentence Game:** Use the word ______ in a sentence.

**Find A Word Story Game:** Find the word ______ on page ____.

**Read A Sentence Game:** Read the (first, second, third...) sentence on page _____.

**Answer Sentence Game:** Find a sentence on this page that tells _________.

**Finish the Sentence Game:** One player or the teacher reads part of a sentence. The player taking the turn finishes the sentence. You may tell the player the page the sentence is on or a choice of two pages.

**Answer a Question Game:** Make up questions to ask about the story that a player must answer before moving on the board.

Answer the questions about *The Ham Dash.*

Ham is in the pan.  

A cat is in the van. 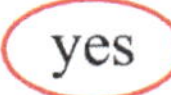 

Dan had a bat.  

Dan sat on the cat.  

The ham lands on a cap.  no

**Sentence Hunt**

Use the book to find the sentences. Fill in the missing word. Write the page number for the sentence.

He ________________ to nab the cat. Page ______

The ham has a ________________. Page ______

The ham gets ________________. Page ______

The ________________ hit the ham. Page ______

3

# Oh, Where is my Cat?

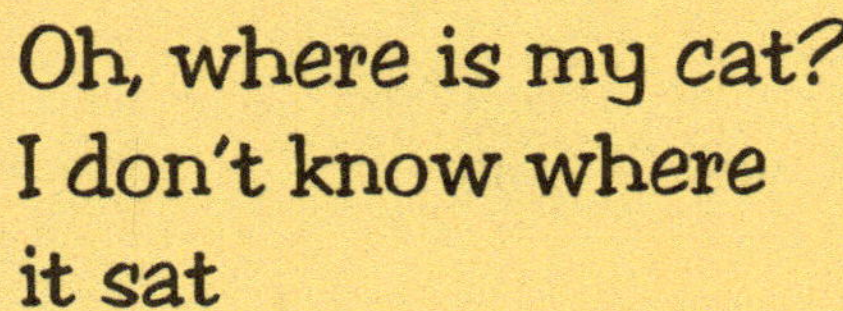

Oh, where is my cat?
I don't know where
it sat

It's not in the grass
or fishing for bass

It's not in the pan
or in a trash can

It's not on a yak
or in a smokestack

It's not on the lamp
or setting up camp

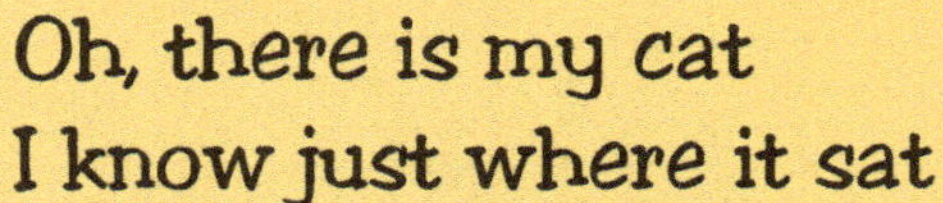

Oh, there is my cat
I know just where it sat

It's there in my cap
just taking a nap

Now , where is my dog?

Answer the questions about *The Green Fig*.

## The Green Fig

The pink hog tips Pam.  yes  no

The dog is quick. yes 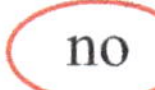 no

The pig bit the dog. yes  no

The dish is the pig's. yes no

The pig can dig a pit.  yes  no

Use the book to find the sentences. Fill in the missing word. Write the page number for the sentence.

The green fig is not in the ________. Page ____

It digs a ________ pit. Page ____

It is in a ________ pit. Page ____

He ________ up the blue dish. Page ____

5

Circle the word the teacher says.

| | | | | | |
|---|---|---|---|---|---|
| 1 | bad | bed | bid | bod | bud |
| 2 | peck | puck | pick | pock | pack |
| 3 | muss | mess | moss | miss | mass |
| 4 | lug | leg | lig | log | lag |
| 5 | pan | pin | pen | pon | pun |

Circle the words that have the same vowel sound as the picture.

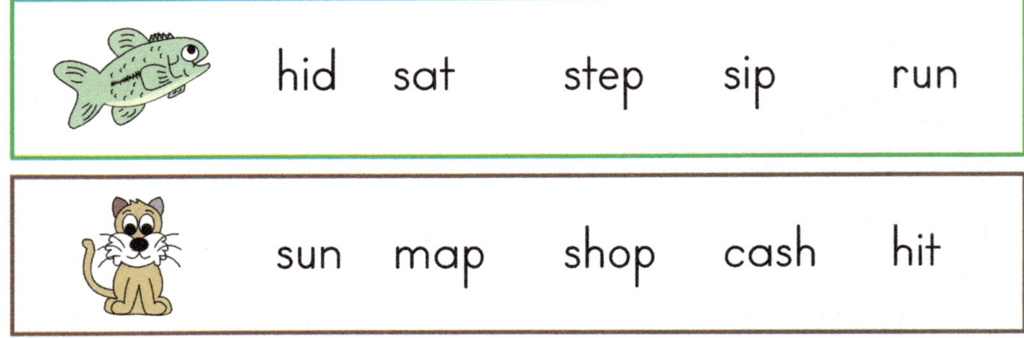


Spelling Test. Write the words the teacher says.

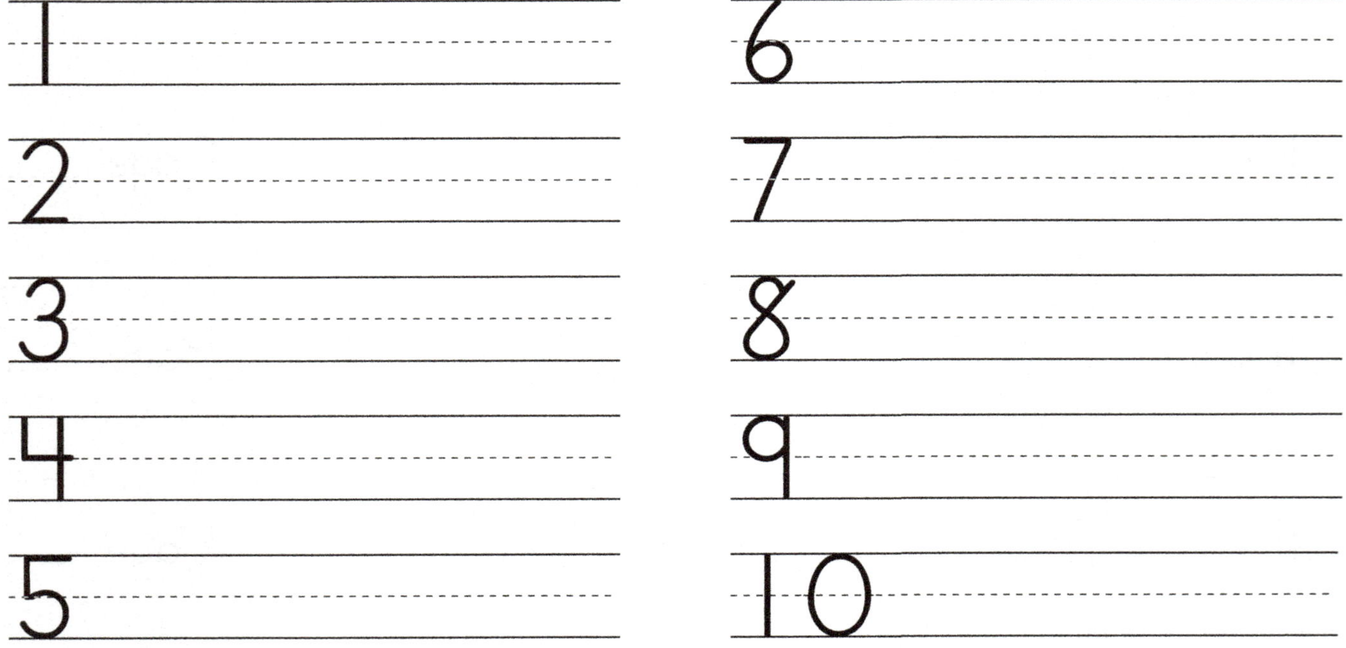

Add *s* to words that mean more than one. Write the words on the lines.

s s

*S* can be added to verbs to match nouns that are not plural (singular). Adding *s* to some verbs makes them singular. Add *s* to the verb spelling words to make them fit the sentences.

cut

The ax ______ big logs.

pull

The man ______ the rope on the bell.

hop

The rabbit ______ into the hole to get away.

8

Answer the questions about *Jed and Bess*.

## Jed and Bess

Jed fell in the well.  yes  no

A duck helped Bess. yes  no

A bell fell in the well. yes 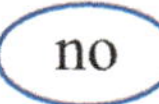 no

Bess pecked the bell. yes  no

Moss is on a rock.  yes  no

Use the book to find the sentences. Fill in the missing word. Write the page number for the sentence.

The ______________ led Bob to Jed. Page ______

Bess ______________ the net. Page ______

The red hen ______________ the cob. Page ______

Jed has the ______________ hen! Page ______

## A Long Necked Pet

If I had a pet
With a very long neck

I could see eggs
In a nest

And red sunsets
In the west

It could rain and yet
I wouldn't get wet

I could hop on a jet
With a single step

On this you could bet
I'd have the very best pet
Oh yes!
If only my pet
Had a very long neck

10

Answer the questions about *The Bug Bus*.

| | | |
|---|---|---|
| The bugs tugged a rug. | yes | no |
| The bugs cut a nut. | yes | no |
| A duck is on the bus. | yes | no |
| Gum is on the bus. | yes | no |
| The bugs hopped in a tub. | yes | no |

The Bug Bus

Bug Bus

Use the book to find the sentences. Fill in the missing word. Write the page number for the sentence.

The bus kicks up ________. Page ____

The bugs ________ to the bus. Page ____

The bugs ________ the jug. Page ____

The bugs ________ a rod. Page ____

 

Circle the word the teacher says.

| | | | | | |
|---|---|---|---|---|---|
| 1 | hid | hed | hod | had | hud |
| 2 | mad | mid | mod | mud | med |
| 3 | teck | tack | tick | tuck | tock |
| 4 | tun | ten | ton | tin | tan |
| 5 | loss | lass | less | liss | luss |

Circle the words that have the same vowel sound as the picture.

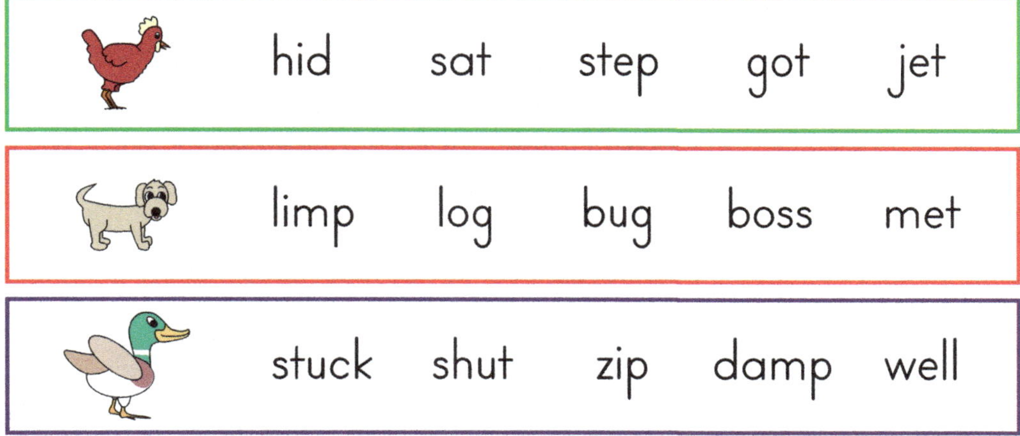


Spelling Test. Write the words the teacher says.

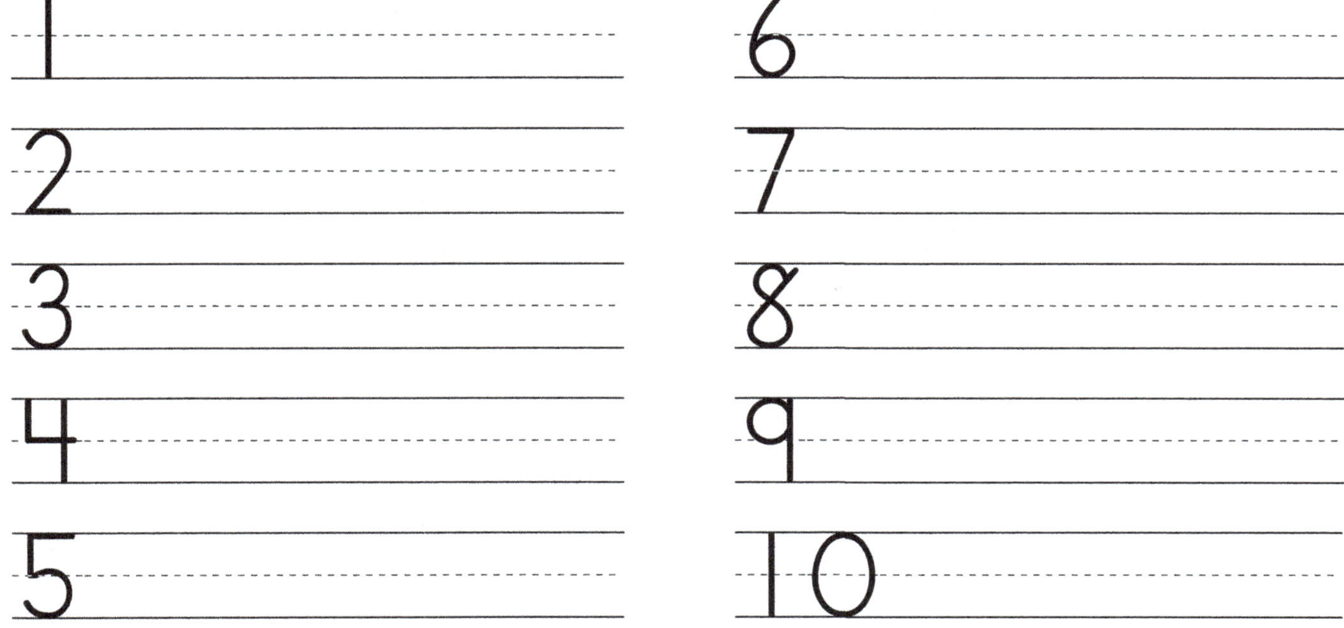

11

A date is written with the month, day, and year.
A comma is used between the day and the year.

September 5, 2012

| |
|---|
| January |
| February |
| March |
| April |
| May |
| June |
| July |
| August |
| September |
| October |
| November |
| December |

Write the dates. Remember to put the comma between the day and year.

Today's date

The first day of the year

The day you were born

Circle the word that best describes the meaning the teacher reads.

1. Say
2. Yell
3. Face
4. Head
5. Shake
6. Bounce
7. Swim
8. Wade
9. Waste
10. Use

 

Find the noun and the verb in each sentence. Fill in the circle to mark your answer.

The ape shakes.

○ noun ○ noun
○ verb ○ verb

The jay ate.

○ noun ○ noun
○ verb ○ verb

The grapes stay.

○ noun ○ noun
○ verb ○ verb

Jane waves.

○ noun ○ noun
○ verb ○ verb

Ray rakes.

○ noun ○ noun
○ verb ○ verb

Dale pays.

○ noun ○ noun
○ verb ○ verb

Add a noun or verb to each sentence. Fill in the circle to mark the kind of word that was added.

| wakes | cape | ape |
|---|---|---|

○ noun ○ verb The ____________ takes grapes.

○ noun ○ verb The babe ____________.

○ noun ○ verb The ____________ faded.

13

Find the list in each sentence. Add commas after the first and second items in the list.

The cat hissed kicked and bit at the dog.

She ate eggs grapes and fish.

The cap is blue red and green.

Wax rags and paste are in the tub.

Circle the word that best describes the meaning the teacher reads.

1. Damp
2. Wet
3. Rest
4. Sleep
5. Step
6. Stomp
7. Rush
8. Race
9. Sad
10. Mad

 

Trace the words. 

The words *are* and *is* are verbs. The word *is* is used in sentences where the noun is one person, place, or thing.

Kate is late.

The word *are* is used in sentences where the noun is more than one person, place, or thing.

Kate and Jay are late.

Fill in the missing word, is or are.

The grapes ______________ purple.

The paste ______________ wasted.

Gabe ______________ awake.

The rakes ______________ on sale.

15

Answer the questions about *Ruff and the Ape*.

## Ruff and the Ape

Gabe ate grapes.  

Ruff lays paste in the cave. yes 

A rake wakes Gabe. yes 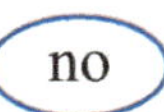

Dale shakes a gate. yes 

A duck gave tape to Ruff.  

Use the book to find the sentences. Fill in the missing word. Write the page number for the sentence.

Dale may not get ________. Page ____

Gabe ________ by the grapes. Page ____

Ruff sat in the ________. Page ____

He ________ Ruff a cake. Page ____

 

18

Read the story. Fill in the spelling words. Choose one of the words by each numbered set of lines.

shore loaf robe goat soak hose roar woke boast pole

One day, a __1__ __2__ mom up. "Time to feed the cat," she said. At last it was my first time to take care of the cat. I put on a __3__. I put a __4__ roast and a __5__ in a pan. I used a __6__ to push the pan. I used a __7__ to fill a tub.

"I can feed the biggest cat," I like to __8__.

roar / loaf 1 __________

bone / hose 5 __________

pole / woke 2 __________

pole / robe 6 __________

boast / robe 3 __________

roar / hose 7 __________

goat / shore 4 __________

boast / soak 8 __________

20

Name: ______________________

**Phonics Test:** Circle the word the teacher says.

| | | | | | |
|---|---|---|---|---|---|
| 1 | soad | soap | sobe | soque | sake |
| 2 | mole | mone | nore | mare | more |
| 3 | rake | rack | roke | rock | roak |
| 4 | cot | coat | cat | cate | koat |
| 5 | store | sore | stare | stone | star |

**Language Test:** Circle the word matches the description the teacher gives you.

| | | | | |
|---|---|---|---|---|
| 1 | doze | toad | soap | vote |
| 2 | oar | oak | oat | oh |
| 3 | poke | mole | boat | toast |
| 4 | home | mode | sole | yoke |
| 5 | roast | note | stone | foam |

 

Answer the questions about *No Toast.*

## No Toast

| | | |
|---|---|---|
| A boar drove a bus. | yes | no |
| A mole was on the stove. | yes | no |
| A goat stole toast. | yes | no |
| Ruff put a bone in a toaster. | yes | no |
| Violet roped the goat. | yes | no |

Use the book to find the sentences. Fill in the missing word. Write the page number for the sentence.

Violet put __________ on the smoke. Page _____

"We will go to the __________". Page _____

It fell over the goat's __________. Page _____

Violet will make a mud __________. Page _____

21

Find the list in each sentence. Add commas after all items in the list except the last.

We fed sheep pigs ducks and deer.

In the bag are red green blue yellow and purple socks.

A dish made of rice beef eggs and green stuff is on the stove.

A coat socks cap and a robe are in the box.

Tom Ann Bev Ron and Dad are in the van.

Circle the word that best describes the meaning the teacher reads.

1. Beef
2. Roast
3. Push
4. Poke
5. Like
6. Love
7. Ship
8. Boat
9. Growl
10. Roar

Find the list in each sentence. Add commas after all items in the list except the last.

The nice big brown mule rested.

I rode a bus boat jet and bike.

I will paste a one three six and five on the page.

The cupcakes had blue white brown and pink icing.

Fish hens snakes and ducks lay eggs.

Circle the word that best describes the meaning the teacher reads.

| | |
|---|---|
| 1. Big | 2. Huge |
| 3. Bus | 4. Van |
| 5. Wish | 6. Hope |
| 7. Grass | 8. Hay |
| 9. Pup | 10. Dog |

# 23

Answer the questions about *Beep.*

Beep was a sheep.  

The rag made Beep sad. 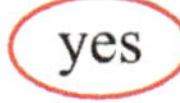 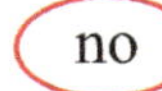

The sheep drove the jeep. 

June paid five dimes for Beep.  

The mice dived into weeds. 

**Sentence Hunt**

Use the book to find the sentences. Fill in the missing word. Write the page number for the sentence.

"My sheep Beep ________," said June. Page ____

"I will make a ________. Do not beep!" Page ____

June hired a ________ vet to cure Beep. Page ____

He spoke ________ most of the time. Page ____

 

Listen to the poem as the teacher reads it to you.

Use the clues to find the spelling words. A list is in the orange box.

time steel huge bite deep size cube seed mule tire

It can rust.

It's bad to go flat.

It may make a weed.

You can ride it.

A big size

A box shape

25

Circle the word the teacher says.

| | | | | | |
|---|---|---|---|---|---|
| 1 | shake | stake | shave | shine | shack |
| 2 | sheek | soak | seek | sick | seem |
| 3 | greed | gripe | gray | grape | grade |
| 4 | maze | note | nine | huge | nose |
| 5 | roll | ride | ruse | rule | reel |
| 6 | rose | roast | boast | roads | grove |
| 7 | pave | bay | paste | pay | page |
| 8 | so | sob | soe | hose | see |

Circle the word that has the same vowel sound as the picture.

| | | | | | |
|---|---|---|---|---|---|
| | race | pile | meet | lute | pose |
| | kite | game | mute | rope | sheet |
| | grace | beep | dine | green | tube |
| | fuse | quote | waste | hive | feel |
| | male | size | tune | foam | steel |

 

Fill in the missing 's in the blanks.
Write the missing words on the lines.

The queen _ _ ________ ate the oats.

Is a goat in Mike _ _ ________ ?

May I ride Jane _ _ ________ ?

Did the ape take June _ _ ________ ?

Dave _ _ ________ is in the cave.

Listen to the poem as the teacher reads it to you.

### Spick-and-Span

I made the kitchen spick-and-span
I washed the plates, I washed the pans

Then I got hungry for a snack
And soon all the mess had come back

So off into my room I snuck
I pushed too hard and pressed my luck

Mom said she doesn't like to nag
But my cleaning had hit a snag

So I had a new mess to face
I wished I was in outer space

But soon all the chores were done
Now my stomach had earned some fun

And so the mess began again
When I clean house I just can't win

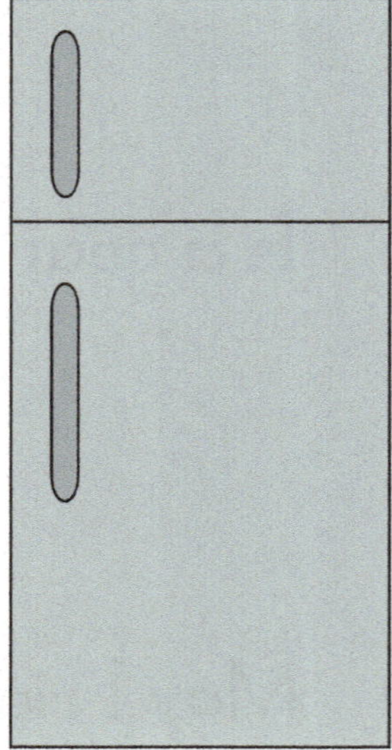

Each sentence is missing a word. Add an apostrophe and *s* to the words above the lines. Write the words in the sentences with apostrophe *s*. Read the sentences.

snake

Did the cat get the __________ snack?

Pat

The spill made a blue spot on __________ rug.

Kate

The red spade is __________.

 

Circle the word the teacher says.

| | | | | | |
|---|---|---|---|---|---|
| 1 | spade | space | snack | speck | spice |
| 2 | spine | mine | snip | pine | span |
| 3 | spice | snack | poke | spike | spoke |
| 4 | stab | snod | snob | snub | spot |
| 5 | nip | snap | spin | pin | snip |
| 6 | spell | spill | pill | snell | sell |
| 7 | snap | snug | stab | span | snag |
| 8 | speed | spike | spoke | speck | snack |

Circle the word that rhymes with each picture.

| | | | | |
|---|---|---|---|---|
| mike | spike | spice | spine | snip |
| spoke | dump | snack | dust | snuck |
| snug | spine | snag | snob | sped |
| spit | snag | spite | spike | speck |
| spot | spat | snap | snip | spit |

Answer the questions about *Spice and Mice.*

## Spice and Mice

The snake ate Kate.  yes  no

The snake liked spice. yes  no

Kate put a vine on the snake. yes 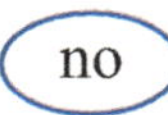 no

The snake had to spin home. yes 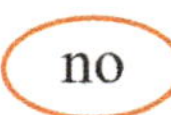 no

Kate rode on the snake's back.  yes  no

## Sentence Hunt

Use the book to find the sentences. Fill in the missing word. Write the page number for the sentence.

"May I __________ the vine on your tail?" Page ______

"__________ and mice can be nice." Page ______

"__________ a vine," spat the snake. Page ______

"I must go," __________ Kate. Page ______

 

Listen as the teacher reads to you about snails.

## Snails

A snail is a gastropod. Gastro means stomach. Pod means foot. A snail has a foot coming out of its stomach. There are many kinds of snails. Some live on land. Most kinds live only in the water.

A snail can hide its head in its shell. It can even seal up its shell when it gets too dry in the summer or too cold in the winter.

Long tubes come out of their heads. These are called tentacles. Snails that live on land have eyes at the end of the tentacles. Water snails have their eyes at the bottom of the tentacles. Some snails have two more tentacles. These are used for smelling.

Land snails dig holes in the ground to hide their eggs. They can lay over one hundred at a time. When the snails hatch, their shells are very soft. They eat their own egg shells to make their body shells stronger. The egg shells contain calcium. Calcium makes their shells strong just like it makes our bones strong. We get calcium from milk and other diary products like cheese and yogurt.

Most snails eat leaves and fruit. If you had a pet snail, it would eat just about anything. If you like plants, you may not like snails. They can destroy farmer's crops. Lots of things eat snails. Frogs, fish, even some kinds of bugs eat snails. People eat a snail dish called escargot. Does a snack of buttery snails sound good to you?

Use the clues to find the spelling words. A list is in the orange box.

stain bait paid waist laid mail tail nail grain snail

| | |
|---|---|
| By hips | It is not fast. |
| Gave cash | A spot on a coat |
| Seeds | Stamps are on it. |

34

Homophones are words that sound alike, but have different meanings.
Below are homophones based on words from the spelling list.
Use the picture clues to help tell the difference between the words.

Write the correct homophone in each sentence. Choices are in the green boxes.

| | |
|---|---|
| Do not ________ the bait.<br>The grass is ________ deep. | waist and waste |
| The pup is a ________.<br>A stamp is on the ________. | male and mail |
| The cat has a fuzzy ________.<br>Will you tell me a funny ________? | tale and tail |

 

Circle the word the teacher says.

| | | | | | |
|---|---|---|---|---|---|
| 1 | jell | jail | jale | gail | gale |
| 2 | maize | mazz | maaze | miaze | maz |
| 3 | paim | pian | pin | pan | pain |
| 4 | am | ann | ame | aim | amy |
| 5 | rad | braid | raid | rid | road |
| 6 | van | bain | wain | vian | vain |
| 7 | grait | gate | gait | grain | gain |
| 8 | naly | nail | nial | name | wail |

Circle the word that sounds the same as the word in the box.

| | | | | | |
|---|---|---|---|---|---|
| male | mall | mial | mail | mayl | may |
| waste | waist | paste | wait | vaist | waits |
| tale | toam | tall | tial | trail | tail |
| sale | sal | sail | sell | say | soil |
| pale | paid | pave | pain | pail | paill |

35

Answer the questions about *Snuff the Snail.*

## Snuff the Snail

Snuff had a pain in his nose.  

The snail hid in a mail box.  

The fish ate the snail.  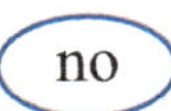

Rain fell on the snail.  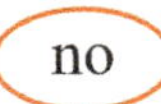

Nails fell in the pail.  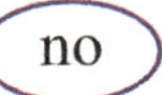

Sentence 

Use the book to find the sentences. Fill in the missing word. Write the page number for the sentence.

The man fed the ________ to the pig. Page ____

Snuff had to race to get off the ________. Page ____

"It is a shame you did not ________." Page ____

The ________ made the snail wail. Page ____

 

Use the clues to find the spelling words. A list is in the orange box.

brave brake broke breeze brush train trip tree trade truck

Use it on hair

It has tires.

Use it to stop

Needs to be fixed

It makes sticks.

It runs on a rail.

Write the words that complete the rhymes.
Choose from the words in the box.

brake tray tree trap

Bruce did not get a map.
He fell into a ________.

The truck had no ________.
It drove into the lake.

It got so big just for me.
I like to sit in the ________.

The cup was on the ________.
It was yellow, blue, and gray.

39

Answer the questions about *Brad the Brat.*

| | | |
|---|---|---|
| Brad put a brush on a track. | yes | no |
| Brad broke Tom's truck. | yes | no |
| Brad put a frog on a tray. | yes | no |
| Brad hid in the brush. | yes | no |
| Brad paid for a truck. | yes | no |

Brad the Brat

Use the book to find the sentences. Fill in the missing word. Write the page number for the sentence.

"That Brad has bad ________," said Trish. Page ____

"I will not put a ________ on the track." Page ____

"My truck is in the ________." Page ____

"May I take the ________ for you?" Page ____

 

Circle the word the teacher says.

| | | | | | |
|---|---|---|---|---|---|
| 1 | bass | grass | brass | brazz | brase |
| 2 | trump | tromp | trop | tomp | tump |
| 3 | braze | braie | brase | brake | brace |
| 4 | bim | brom | rim | brim | brime |
| 5 | trike | trick | tick | track | rick |
| 6 | truck | tuck | track | tack | truke |
| 7 | bribe | brid | bide | brite | bride |
| 8 | trim | tim | time | trime | trin |

Circle the word that rhymes with the picture in the box.

| | | | | | |
|---|---|---|---|---|---|
| | brain | track | rail | came | trash |
| | bran | trod | bray | tred | trot |
| | brad | brat | trap | brake | trim |
| | trash | brush | Bruce | Trish | trick |
| 6 | trips | brims | tricks | brace | traps |

## 43

Write the missing words.
Choose from the words in the box.

| away | afraid | awake | across | agree |
|---|---|---|---|---|

The frog was ______________ of the snake.

Fran put ______________ the dress.

The crab ran ______________ the road.

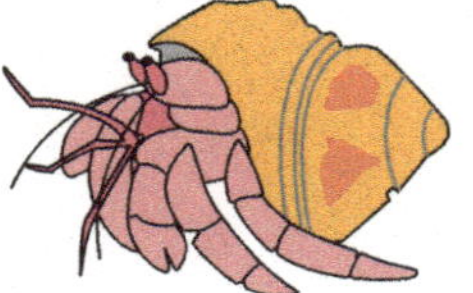

Did Craig ______________ to pay the price?

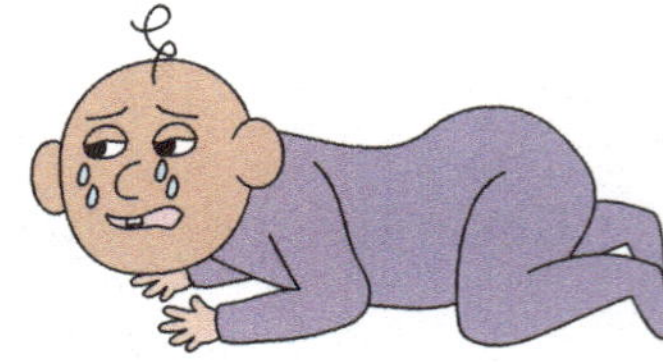

Did the baby keep mom ______________?

Use the clues to find the spelling words. A list is in the orange box.

| creek | praise | drain | across | prize | fry | crush | dress | freeze | press |
|---|---|---|---|---|---|---|---|---|---|

Use a hot pan ______________

Tromp on a can ______________

Win it ______________

A mom puts it on. ______________

Open a hole ______________

Make into ice ______________

 

Listen to the poem as the teacher reads it to you.

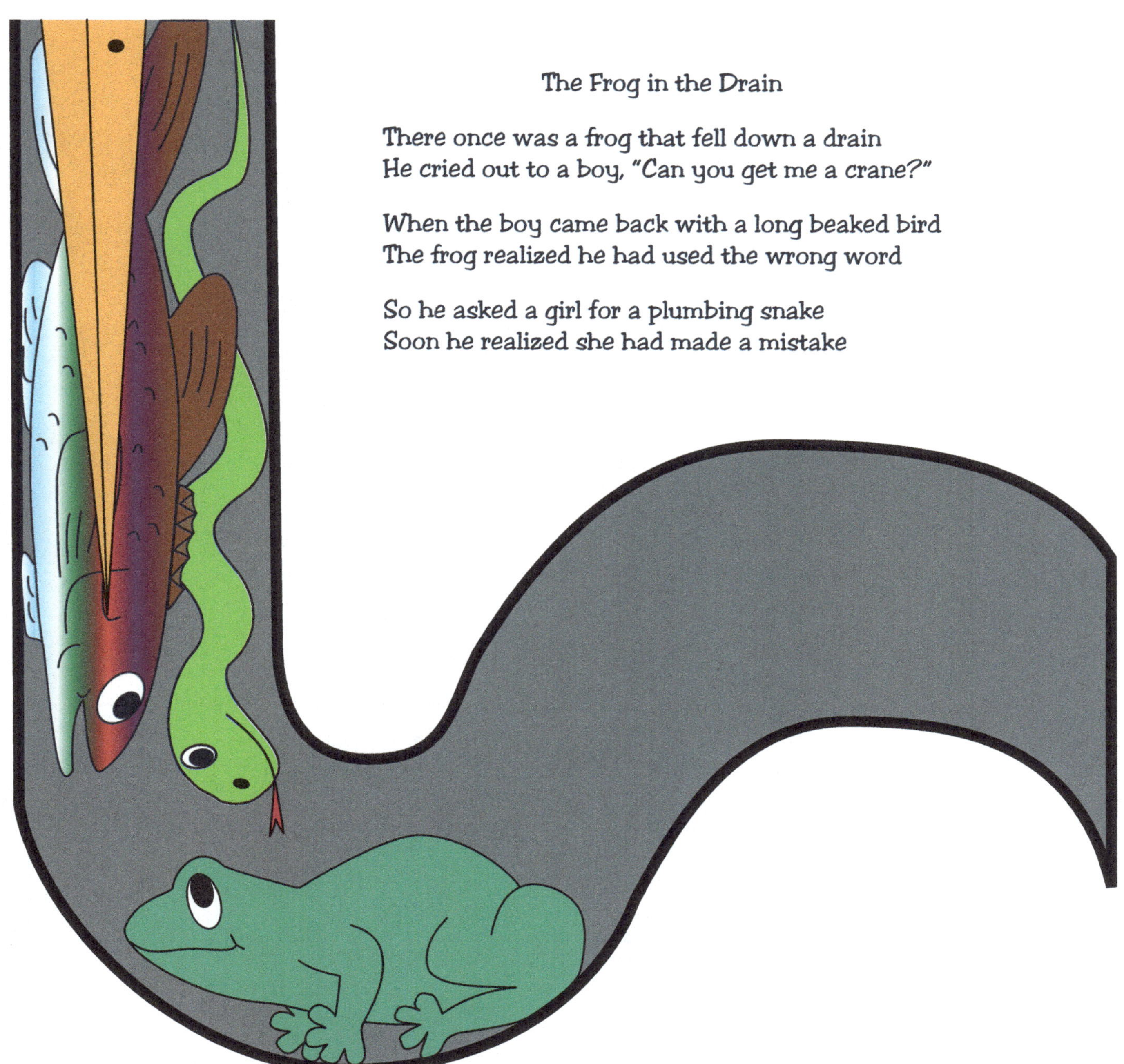

The Frog in the Drain

There once was a frog that fell down a drain
He cried out to a boy, "Can you get me a crane?"

When the boy came back with a long beaked bird
The frog realized he had used the wrong word

So he asked a girl for a plumbing snake
Soon he realized she had made a mistake

Next he asked a man, "Can you fish me out?"
What he got instead was a rainbow trout

The unhappy frog cried, "Will you hear my plea?
"And send me some help that won't eat me!"

In his frustration he let out a croak.
The sound was so loud the drain pipe broke

45

Circle the word the teacher says.

| | | | | | |
|---|---|---|---|---|---|
| 1 | cave | crave | brave | rave | craze |
| 2 | drill | brill | drile | prill | dill |
| 3 | fast | frast | lost | frogs | frost |
| 4 | prime | ride | pride | prick | pide |
| 5 | crie | shy | kry | cry | cri |
| 6 | prop | dry | drove | drop | broke |
| 7 | price | prick | pric | pice | prize |
| 8 | frade | fray | awake | across | afraid |

Circle the word that rhymes with the picture.

| | | | | | |
|---|---|---|---|---|---|
| | pride | drip | crab | prop | agree |
| | drug | frog | prize | crest | drip |
| | free | press | freeze | creek | creed |
| | frail | crush | praise | Fran | crane |
| 5 | pray | fry | drive | dry | crave |

Answer the questions about *Fred the Frog*.

## Fred the Frog

| | | |
|---|---|---|
| Fred had a frog named Craig. | yes | no |
| The frog made a hole in the wall. | yes | no |
| The frog sat on prunes. | yes | no |
| The frog hopped into a crib. | yes | no |
| The frog hid in a dress. | yes | no |

Use the book to find the sentences. Fill in the missing word. Write the page number for the sentence.

The frog made Dad drop the ________. Page ____

Craig stuck the frog in a ________. Page ____

"Do not ________ the frog!" said Mom. Page ____

"I must ________ this dress," said Sis. Page ____

48

Read the sentences. Find the nouns and the verb in each sentence. Write the nouns on the red lines. Write the verb on the blue lines.

Fran made the dress.

Fran dress

made

The dog barked at the horse.

The car parked on two arms.

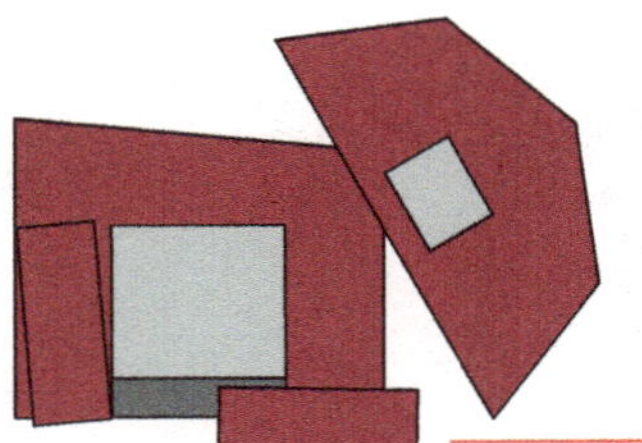

A storm hit the barn.

Unscramble the sentences and write them on the lines.

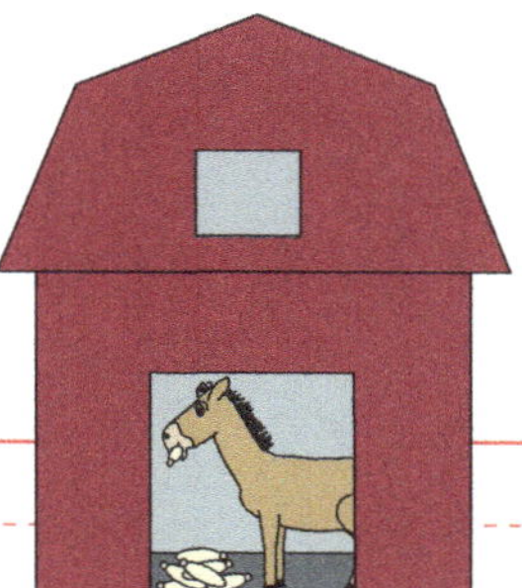

horse ate the barn in the corn the.

shorts wore orange the shark.

Use the clues to find the spelling words. A list is in the orange box.

dark corn shark barn horse storm yard short large morning

Rain

Part of a day

Not tall

It has fins.

On a cob

You can ride it.

50

Circle the word the teacher says.

| | | | | | |
|---|---|---|---|---|---|
| 1 | card | corn | carve | cart | cork |
| 2 | fort | fork | for | form | force |
| 3 | mark | more | nor | morn | mart |
| 4 | stare | star | store | start | stork |
| 5 | tore | tare | torn | turn | tart |
| 6 | yard | your | yarn | yor | yes |
| 7 | dark | dart | bark | barn | dorm |
| 8 | are | ore | ark | art | arm |

Circle the word that matches the picture in the box.

| | | | | |
|---|---|---|---|---|
| | hark | store | carp | torn |
| | arm | hard | stork | yarn |
| Jam | fort | short | card | jar |
| | park | star | sharp | lard |
| | yard | bar | shark | shore |

 

Answer the questions about *At Home on the Farm.*

| | | |
|---|---|---|
| Kate is Nate's wife. | yes | no |
| A goat ate a steel sheet. | yes | no |
| A sheep is named Bart. | yes | no |
| The sheep bumped the log. | yes | no |
| The mice bit the sheep. | yes | no |

At Home on the Farm

Use the book to find the sentences. Fill in the missing word. Write the page number for the sentence.

The goat ran to the ________. Page ____

Kate and Nate are not ________. Page ____

"It will be bad if it ________," said a sheep. Page ____

The home is a ________ log. Page ____

53

Read the clues. Find the vowel + r word from the word list that answers the clue. Write the answers in the boxes. Look at the arrows to decide if the words should be written down or across.

**Across**

2. Mix it up
4. Hair of a dog
5. You put it on.
6. It can make you sick.
7. A fire will do this.
8. You can dig it.
9. Helps the sick

**Down** 

1. Pop
3. A cat can do this.
4. 1st
5. Ride a wave.
6. She is a ______
7. Its home is a nest.

| dirt | purr | burn | surf | shirt | nurse | stir |
|---|---|---|---|---|---|---|
| first | girl | fur | bird | burst | germ | |

Fill in the missing words in the sentences.

The girl lost her ____________ in the store.

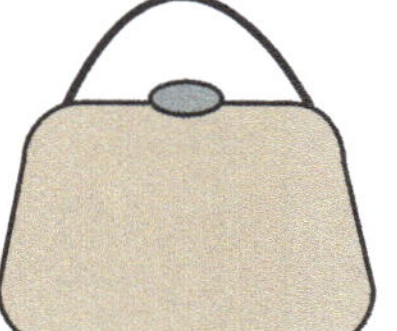

The dirt got on the ____________.

The ____________ put her yarn in her nest.

Use the clues to find the spelling words. A list is in the orange box.

turn every girl burst were shirt bird curve nurse first

Was ____________

Takes care of the sick ____________

Bend ____________

Steer a truck ____________

Not a boy ____________

It can lay eggs. ____________

Not last ____________

Need it to get dressed ____________

55

Circle the word the teacher says.

| | | | | | |
|---|---|---|---|---|---|
| 1 | Bert | bun | burn | burr | bird |
| 2 | curt | corn | carl | carp | curl |
| 3 | nurse | nerves | must | nursery | nor |
| 4 | stirred | shirt | shin | sure | short |
| 5 | wore | ware | wire | were | worse |
| 6 | her | herd | hard | hurt | hot |
| 7 | gene | joke | gem | jerk | germ |
| 8 | farm | form | fur | firm | fir |

Circle the word that rhymes with the picture.

| | | | | | |
|---|---|---|---|---|---|
| | bark | burn | term | yarn | torn |
| | card | nor | stir | her | star |
| | nurse | harsh | burst | purr | first |
| | verse | force | hose | sore | horn |
| | Kirk | lord | herd | yard | stir |

Answer the questions about *Super Pork Makes Friends*.

| | | |
|---|---|---|
| Mort had a pen by the barn. | yes | no |
| Barb helped Mort. | yes | no |
| The birds gave Mort a cape. | yes | no |
| The shirt was too small for Mort. | yes | no |
| The pig made a fort. | yes | no |

Super Pork Makes Friends

Use the book to find the sentences. Fill in the missing word. Write the page number for the sentence.

"Do not get ________ on me," Page ____

They got a ________ and yarn. Page ____

"It is too far up the ________ tree." Page ____

"I will poke you with my ________," Page ____

 

Read the sentences. Choose the word that is or isn't a contraction to make the sentence match the picture. Write the correct word on the lines.

The dog ______________ standing on the box.

is isn't

The birds ______________ on the pig.

are aren't

The steel bar ______________ bend.

did didn't

The horses ______________ in a truck.

are aren't

The king ______________ singing a song.

is isn't

The frog ______________ sit on the rock.

did didn't

 

Circle the word the teacher says.

| | | | | | |
|---|---|---|---|---|---|
| 1 | isnot | isn't | ins't | isnt | is |
| 2 | wating | wanting | want | wantn'g | wants |
| 3 | wing | sing | vine | zig | zing |
| 4 | band | banging | bang | ban | bant |
| 5 | print | pin | ping | pend | pint |
| 6 | brand | band | brond | bran | bad |
| 7 | lend | let | len't | lent | led |
| 8 | saint | sant | sante | santa | sat |

Circle the word that completes the sentence.

The truck is ______________ a horse.
bring and bringing can't panting

The dog ______________ bark at the birds.
didn't barking isn't dent din't

Barb will ______________ the painting.
aren't hanging hung sung hang

Did a bee ______________ your hand?
sang sting ant stung sing

The frogs ______________ afraid of the fish.
weren't werent wern't worn wing

61

Read the sentence. One sentence has two words switched. One sentence is correct. Put a C in the box before the correct sentence. Put an X in the box before the incorrect sentence.

☐ The stain made a dark spill.
☐ The spill made a dark stain.

☐ Did Bert spill the nails?
☐ Did Bert nails the spill?

☐ The snake hurt its tail.
☐ The tail hurt its snake.

☐ The spot fell in one rain.
☐ The rain fell in one spot.

☐ Bruce had to wait for his snack.
☐ Bruce had to snack for his wait.

Put the frogs in alphabetical order. Number them from 1 to 5.

mail paid spill wait grain

Put the snails in alphabetical order. Number them from 1 to 5.

snail bait nail rain tail

 

Read each sentence. One word needs an apostrophe. Put the apostrophe where it belongs. In the box at the beginning of the sentence put a B if the apostrophe was used to show that something belonged to something else. Put a C if the apostrophe was used in a contraction.

☐ The tree isn t too large.

☐ Trish can drive Brad s truck.

☐ The horses weren t afraid of Fred.

☐ The frog was jumping into Carl s creek.

☐ Bruce and Barn aren t alone at the camp.

☐ Craig s prize was a free train ride.

☐ Fran didn t drop the drums.

☐ The crane s wings are large.

 

63

Read the story.

One day a bird come to a barn. It made a nest in a cart.
The bird laid three eggs in the nest.
"We will take the cart to the store," said Kirk to his horse, Carl.
He led the horse to the cart. But, the bird began singing.
"Do not be afraid," said Kirk to the bird. "Do not go away.
We aren't going to take the cart. I will take my truck."
So, the bird's nest was safe.

Fill in the answer to the sentences yes or no.

2. The bird made a nest in a cart.
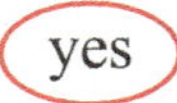

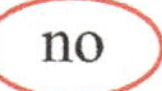


3. The bird had three eggs.

4. Did Kirk take the cart?

5. The horse began singing.

Read the sentences. Fill in the circle next to the word that completes the sentence.

The ______ made a tick tock sound.

- O crock
- O clock
- O cloak

A ______ is like a map.

- O globe
- O glob
- O glode

The girls ate the purple ______.

- O plumps
- O plums
- O plumes

I will be ______ if I win first prize.

- O glob
- O glade
- O glad

Did Clark ride on the big ______?

- O plane
- O plan
- O play

Read the words. Circle the words with the long *i* sound.
Put an X on the words that do not have a long *i* sound.

| bind | king | find | hint | grind |
|---|---|---|---|---|
| mint | mind | sting | kind | sing |

Read the sentences. Fill in the circle next to the word that completes the sentence.

_______ of the big dog.

- O Began
- O Befriend
- O Beware

Glen hid _______ the rock.

- O behind
- O behave
- O before

Clark was not _______ too nice.

- O beside
- O being
- O begun

Is it time to _______ the race?

- O beyond
- O begin
- O betray

The pink glass _______ to me.

- O became
- O begun
- O belongs

Use the clues to find the spelling words. A list is in the orange box.

clock glass plane before play globe close begin glad plate clam became

Start

_______________

It has a shell.

_______________

Have fun

_______________

It is like a bird.

_______________

It ticks.

_______________

A drink is in it.

_______________

Not open

_______________

It is shaped like a ball.

_______________

Sentence Hunt

## Clark's Plane

Use the book to find the sentences.
Fill in the missing word.
Write the page number for the sentence.

The girl began to raise the ______________. Page ______

Clark hid ______________ a large plant. Page ______

"I will ______________ to my mom next time." Page ______

The plates became a big ______________ . Page ______

Read the pairs of sentences. Look at the words in black print. Fill in the circle next to the sentences that uses the bold word as a verb.

- O Is the **plug** in the tub?
- O Will you **plug** in the clock?

- O He will **clip** the tree.
- O I have a red hair **clip**.

- O Can we see a **play**?
- O Can we **play**?

- O Clark will **store** the cans.
- O Clark will go to the **store**.

- O We will camp on that **land**.
- O She will **land** the plane.

- O Clark did not **mind** his mom.
- O My **mind** is in my brain.

Circle the word the teacher says.

| | | | | | |
|---|---|---|---|---|---|
| 1 | claping | clabbing | clapping | clap | capping |
| 2 | begin | began | became | beg | begun |
| 3 | plane | plat | pate | plate | prate |
| 4 | gad | glad | glade | glide | grad |
| 5 | begrind | grin | grine | grand | grind |
| 6 | plug | plunge | plune | plunj | punge |
| 7 | sing | bring | cling | king | clinging |
| 8 | paying | plant | playying | playing | pling |

Fill in the circle next to the word that completes the sentence.

Did you ____________________ a clam?

- ○ find ○ kind ○ behind ○ cling ○ plot

The coat ____________________ to his son.

- ○ began ○ play ○ hitting ○ besides ○ belongs

The dog is ____________________ in the dirt.

- ○ dug ○ digging ○ drag ○ dig ○ dip

A glass and ____________________ are on the tray.

- ○ glass ○ close ○ plate ○ kind ○ betray

Liz was winding the ____________________.

- ○ clock ○ plush ○ grind ○ beware ○ click

 

Read the story.

The flock of ducks flew to the lake. A sly fox hid on the bluff.

"I will slip behind the ducks," said the fox.

He was creeping up on the flock. But, a blond girl came playing her flute. "My hope of getting a duck is slim," said the fox. "The blond girl is to blame. She must flee to her home."

Slumping behind a rock slab, he began to bark. But the girl did not flee. She saw the fox, "You must like my flute. It made you sing."

"See the singing fox," the blond girl said to the flock. The flock did see the sly fox. The ducks flew away.

"You are to blame. Your blabbing made the ducks flee," said the fox.

"I have a nice slice of cake," said the girl. The fox and girl ate cake.

"I was wanting duck," said the fox. "But, cake is nice too."

Fill in the answer to the sentences yes or no.

1. A sly dog hid on the bluff. yes no

2. The girl was playing a flute. yes no

3. The fox ate the ducks. yes no

4. The fox made the girl flee. yes no

5. The fox and girl ate cake. yes no

Read the clues. Find the word from the word list that answers the clue or completes the sentence. Write the answers in the boxes. Look at the arrows to decide if the words should be written down or across.

**Across**

1. It can cut.
2. It sounds like sick.
3. You can ride it in snow.
4. If you get a cut, you may _____.
5. You lay on a bed to _____.
6. A tire with a hole in it
7. A big fire
8. You can play on it.

**Down** 

1. It can float.
2. A _____ of geese.
3. It is part of a coat.
5. It can cut.
6. You can wave it.
7. Can't see
9. Not fat

| flag | sled | bleed | blind | sleep | blimp | flat | sleeve |
|---|---|---|---|---|---|---|---|
| blaze | slim | flock | blade | slide | saw | flick | |

 

Answer the questions about *Blaze and the Flock.*

Geese froze to the lake.  

Blaze is a duck.  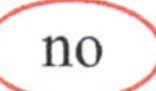

Blaze has a saw and sled.  

Blaze made a blimp.  

A duck got in a sling shot.  

Blaze and the Flock

Use the book to find the sentences. Fill in the missing word. Write the page number for the sentence.

"Your feet ________ in the ice." Page ____

The duck was a ________ as it slid on the ice. Page ____

Blaze began ________ ropes on the blimp. Page ____

The flock began ________ their wings. Page ____

75

Circle the word the teacher says.

| | | | | | |
|---|---|---|---|---|---|
| 1 | blapping | blabbing | blabing | babbing | baping |
| 2 | fuff | fluff | luff | flaff | floff |
| 3 | slid | side | sid | slibe | slide |
| 4 | sleeve | seeve | sleewe | steer | steve |
| 5 | fish | fesh | flesh | flees | first |
| 6 | sing | sling | song | slin | slug |
| 7 | last | fast | blest | blast | best |
| 8 | flick | floss | floke | flock | flew |

Fill in the circle next to the word that completes the sentence.

Can you fly in a ______________________ a clam?

○ fly ○ flee ○ blimp ○ blaze ○ slim

The ______________________ is on a pole.

○ sly ○ flax ○ salt ○ blot flag

The black dog is ______________________.

○ sleeping ○ seep ○ sleep ○ steep seeming

Ice made the road ______________________.

○ sick ○ slick ○ slack ○ slim stick

Did the cut on your hand ______________________?

○ sling ○ blade ○ flesh ○ bleed ○ saw

 

Rewrite the words above the sentences as contractions.

Let us

__________ rest on the bank of the creek.

It is

__________ fun to skip and hop.

He is

__________ drinking his milk.

She is

__________ asking her mom for a scarf.

Read each sentence. Look at the name with the apostrophe.
If the name is a contraction, put a C in the box at the beginning of the sentence.
If it shows something belongs to it, put a B in the box.

- ☐ Mike's dog is walking.
- ☐ Mike's walking a dog.

- ☐ Jane's skirt is green.
- ☐ Jane's putting on a green skirt.

- ☐ Violet's skating on the lake.
- ☐ Violet's skates fell in the lake.

- ☐ Hank's truck is honking.
- ☐ Hank's honking the horn on his truck.

 

78

Read the sentences. Write the number under the picture that matches it.

1. The deer is between the crates.
2. The crate is behind the deer.
3. The deer is beside the crate.
4. The deer is inside the crate.
5. The deer is over the crate.
6. The deer is under the crate.

Read the sentences. Use the description of how they spoke as a clue and write the name of the character speaking.

Fran

Hal

Liz

Jill

Fluff

Bess

Jed

Gus

"I napped under the tree," purred __________.

"I am hunting for deer," roared __________.

"I need help!" barked __________.

"Is my egg in the nest? quacked __________.

"I banged my nose on the gate," grunted __________.

"Is the seed in the dirt?" peeped __________.

"Is a fox in the barn?" clucked __________.

"I jumped into the pond," croaked __________.

80

Circle the word the teacher says.

| | | | | | |
|---|---|---|---|---|---|
| 1 | trunk | tunk | trank | trun | trung |
| 2 | tall | stalk | talk | take | tolk |
| 3 | sared | stared | scard | scaring | scared |
| 4 | shirt | skirt | spurt | skurt | skirm |
| 5 | asked | tasking | elking | asking | ashed |
| 6 | skiding | skidded | slidding | skided | skidding |
| 7 | risk | brisk | bisk | bresk | brisck |
| 8 | brisket | bask | basket | basked | bashed |

Fill in the circle next to the word that completes the sentence.

________________ drink the pink stuff.

○ Didn't ○ Drank ○ Scuff ○ Don't ○ Silk

The trunk was big and ________________.

○ bulky ○ wink ○ crank ○ bulk ○ walk

She's ________________ the horn on the bus.

○ hank ○ honking ○ yank ○ scale ○ skated

Frank was ________________ on the steep slope.

○ ski ○ skipped ○ skyed ○ skunk ○ skiing

Violet put the ________________ on her face.

○ pink ○ mask ○ cents ○ sulk ○ shank

 

Listen to the poem as the teacher reads it to you.

## Elephants on Ice

The elephants came to our new ice rink.
But the place was too small is what I think.

The swayed way too much and they loved to twirl
Sweeping aside every boy and each girl

They busted down doors and cracked up the walls
The rink shifts a little each time that one falls.

The elephants left very bad smell
They live with some swine, that you can tell

The wear and tear on the rink had to ease
So I gave them a gift of some fine Swiss cheese.

Though my crafty plan may not have been nice
The elephants left when in came the mice.

Listen to the poem as the teacher reads it to you.

sw blends

sm blends

ft blends

tw blends

Use the book to find the sentences.
Fill in the missing word.
Write the page number
for the sentence.

Emily Rose

Nate was ____________ in the fish tank. Page ______

"But she is so ____________" said Mrs. Rose. Page ______

"I was going to paint a ____________," Page ______

"Emily ____________ me twice with her brush," Page ______

Replace the two words above the lines with a contraction. Fill in the circle next to the correct way to write the contraction.

Elaine is playing on the swing. ○ Elaines ○ Elaine's ○ Elaines'

It is not smart to swim alone. ○ It's ○ Its ○ Is't

Do not fall off the raft. ○ Don't ○ Do'nt ○ D'not

The men were not sweeping the rugs. ○ wer'nt ○ were'nt ○ weren't

Elaine is a smart and sweet girl. ○ Shes ○ Shi's ○ She's

 

Circle the word the teacher says.

| | | | | | |
|---|---|---|---|---|---|
| 1 | sall | tall | tell | stall | stoll |
| 2 | wish | swise | swiss | swosh | swish |
| 3 | smell | mall | sall | small | smull |
| 4 | twin | tin | tween | twime | twine |
| 5 | shifting | sift | shift | sifted | shifted |
| 6 | twirl | tworl | twarl | twirft | twist |
| 7 | smock | smoke | smoce | swoke | smoak |
| 8 | lift | tuff | tuft | tutt | tufting |

Fill in the circle next to the word that completes the sentence.

Can we shop at the ____________?

○ smock ○ mall ○ cleft ○ smog ○ twirl

The new girl in class is ____________.

○ smart ○ smoke ○ swing ○ tweed ○ stall

Can he ____________ the lid on the jar?

○ twig ○ swell ○ hall ○ drift ○ twist

I can ____________ the bat and hit the ball.

○ smug ○ swim ○ rift ○ swing ○ swung

The log ____________ on the lake.

○ lifted ○ drifted ○ shaft ○ sifting ○ drafting

 

87

Write the number after each sentence to match the missing word.

1. front
2. mother's
3. Something
4. son
5. some
6. from
7. come
8. done
9. brother
10. someone

_______ is under my bed. _______

My _______ name is Beth. _______

My _______ hit the ball with the bat. _______

Are you _______ mopping the room? _______

A deer ran in _______ of their car. _______

Will you _______ home with me? _______

Did he get the clothes _______ the box? _______

My brother is my dad's _______. _______

We had _______ milk to drink. _______

Is _______ putting water in the bath tub? _______

 

Match the clues to the body parts. Write the number from the clue on the lines above the body parts.

hair skin nose lips teeth brain neck throat feet legs

1. I can run and jump. I have feet at the end of me.
2. You are using me. I make you think.
3. You pass me to eat. I can give you a kiss.
4. I can turn your face. A throat is inside me.
5. Put socks on me. Take me for a walk.
6. I bite, but I make a nice smile.
7. If you think something stinks, keep it away from me.
8. It's ok to cut me. I can be black, brown, red, blond, or gray.
9. I am inside your neck. Drink and it will get me wet.
10. Put clothes on me. The sun can burn me. I feel things.

Read the sentences. If the word in black print has the voiced *th* sound, put a **V** in the box. If it is unvoiced, put an **U** for unvoiced.

☐ "Don't stray off the **path**," said Dad.

☐ May I have **this** plum?

☐ **These** cars don't belong to me.

☐ Singing made my **throat** dry.

☐ Did you **thank** her for the cloth?

89

Use the book to find the sentences. Fill in the missing word. Write the page number for the sentence.

Thump

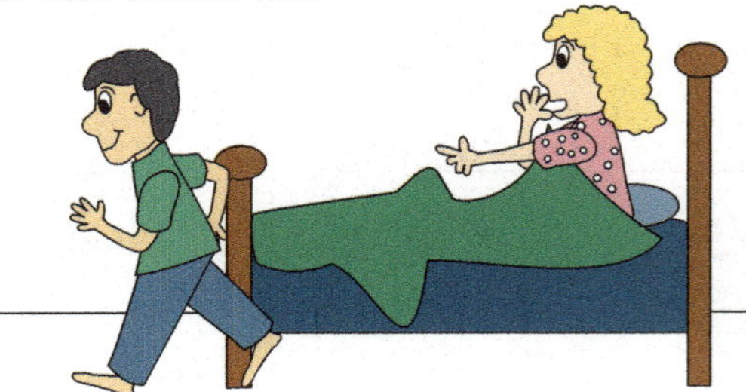

"You didn't do well in ____________. Page ______

"Don't blame your ____________ if you are scared." Page ______

"____________ Thurman is asking for it," said Beth. Page ______

"But, you can't trick your ____________." Page ______

Read the list of words. Complete the sentence to tell how the list is alike. Choose from the words in the red box. Write the number for the word that completes the sentences. Not all words will be used.

____ bus, car, horse, train
Things you can ____.

____ sticks, plums, pine cones, figs
Things that come from ____.

____ cat, dog, mink, skunk
Things that have ____.

____ socks. coat, shirt, skirt, hat
Things that are made of ____.

1. fur 2. moth 3. face 4. trees 5. threes 6. cloth 7. ride 8. from

 

Circle the word the teacher says.

| | | | | | |
|---|---|---|---|---|---|
| 1 | form | foam | from | frim | frame |
| 2 | thin | than | thine | then | tham |
| 3 | bother | broth | sister | father | brother |
| 4 | someone | sumwon | something | some | thing |
| 5 | tha | they | thai | thy | tey |
| 6 | think | than | thang | thank | thunk |
| 7 | teth | teef | theet | teethe | teeth |
| 8 | bathe | bath | bave | bate | bothe |

Fill in the circle next to the word that completes the sentence.

Something fell and made a ___________.

○ thup ○ math ○ thump ○ thorn ○ thus

The fast ride was ___________.

○ thirst ○ those ○ froming ○ thrilling ○ frothed

The ___________ flew to the lamp.

○ thud ○ from ○ these ○ moth ○ they

May we ___________ with you?

○ come ○ going ○ didn't ○ went ○ came

___________ are thinking hard.

○ They ○ Thin ○ Theft ○ Path ○ There

92

Are the words nouns or verbs? Fill in the circles to mark your answers.

| | | | | | |
|---|---|---|---|---|---|
| wolf | O noun | O verb | grow | O noun | O verb |
| scold | O noun | O verb | calf | O noun | O verb |
| help | O noun | O verb | hold | O noun | O verb |
| colt | O noun | O verb | gold | O noun | O verb |
| throw | O noun | O verb | melt | O noun | O verb |
| shelf | O noun | O verb | blow | O noun | O verb |

Read the words. Circle the word in each box that doesn't belong.

| | |
|---|---|
| throw toss pass rock | wolf hold grip held |
| colt slow calf pup | plate glass plums bowl |
| ducks felt geese crows | gulp drink bolt sip |
| frost ice snow fire | plus first third twelfth |

 

Listen to the poem as the teacher reads it to you.

### The Cone That Wasn't Licked

My ice cream cone began to melt
It dribbled on my brand new belt
And in the sun it really flowed
The sidewalk looked like it had snowed

It got so deep it reached our scalps
We had to climb the tall Swiss Alps
And when we reached the very top
The cold air made the melting stop

So all the cones are on a shelf
I locked them there all by myself
I now eat ice cream with one goal
I try to keep it in the bowl

Find the words in the poem that have the blends and digraph. Write the words on the lines.

ow

lf

ld

lt

lp

Answer the questions about *The Wolf That Yelled Crow.*

The Wolf That Yelled Crow

| | | |
|---|---|---|
| Did the wolves eat sweet colts? | yes | no |
| Did Walt gulp a malt? | yes | no |
| Did just two crows get into the corn? | yes | no |
| Was Walt scolded by his mother? | yes | no |
| Did the brother pelt the crows with rocks? | yes | no |

## Sentence Hunt

Use the book to find the sentences. Fill in the missing word. Write the page number for the sentence.

They all worked to __________ the corn. Page _____

Mother and Father wolf __________ him. Page _____

You are __________ malts again. Page _____

He __________ the crows with rocks. Page _____

 

Circle the word the teacher says.

| | | | | | |
|---|---|---|---|---|---|
| 1 | sold | sell | self | selves | shelf |
| 2 | wolves | woves | wolf | wolfs | wolzes |
| 3 | boat | belt | bald | dolt | bolt |
| 4 | low | crow | load | law | glow |
| 5 | flow | flown | fown | flon | frown |
| 6 | gull | gulf | golf | gulp | guld |
| 7 | well | welt | wold | will | weld |
| 8 | sold | scald | scold | skilled | scolded |

Fill in the circle next to the word that completes the sentence.

The ring was made of __________.

O gold O mold O old O cold O sold

Are there grapes in the __________?

O bow O mow O bowling O bowl O tilt

Can the truck __________ the car?

O snow O tow O elf O silt O told

A plant is on the __________.

O wilt O half O scalp O shelf O gown

The hurt girl yelled for __________.

O slow O halt O colt O malt O help

Read each sentence. The words in bold print need one more letter.
Fill in either a *b*, *c*, *f*, *g*, *p*, or *s* to make the correct words.

1. The ___**lane** ___**lided** in the sky.
2. ___**lack** paint was on my ___**leeve.**
3. We smashed the ___**lay** to make it ___**lat.**
4. Did you find a ___**lace** to hang the ___**lock**?
5. If you ___**lice** your hand it may ___**leed.**

Read the sentences with missing words.
Write the number of the sentence on the lines next to the missing word.

___ behind ___ scarf ___ smell ___ skunk

___ throat ___ twig ___ swimming

1. We were ____ in the lake.
2. We can ____ the roses.
3. The red ____ was on my neck.
4. The ____ made our camp stink.
5. My ____ was sore.
6. The ____ came from an oak tree.
7. Is an elk ____ the rock?

 

Write contractions for the pairs of words.

1. it is
2. father is
3. are not
4. he is
5. Beth is
6. she is

Match the description to the picture. Write the number.

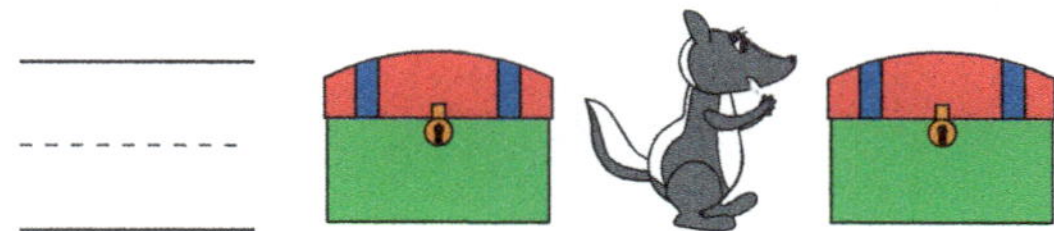

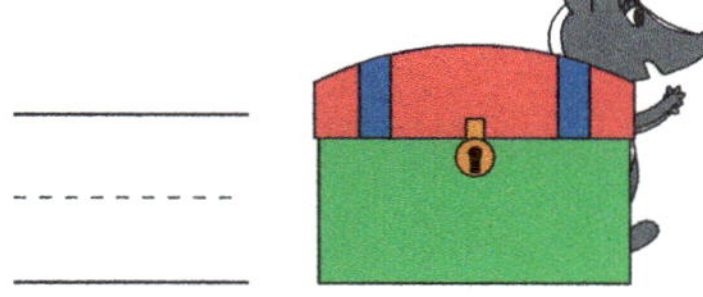

1. The skunk is behind the trunk.
2. The skunk is over the trunk.
3. The skunk is between the trunks.
4. The skunk is under the trunk.
5. The skunk is inside the trunk.
6. The skunk is beside the trunk.

# 97

Read each sentence. Write in the missing word. Choose words from the list. Not all words will be used.

1. I can't ____________ the ball.

2. Hank is ____________ to his dog.

3. The desk is ____________ the wall.

4. Did Frank ____________ up the toy hen?

5. I will ____________ my mom.

**List**

| | |
|---|---|
| grind | behind |
| kind | blind |
| mind | wind |
| find | hind |

Choose the words that complete the sentences. Match the number from the sentence to the word.

| | | | |
|---|---|---|---|
| ____ rink | ____ ask | ____ honked | ____ desk |
| ____ milk | ____ talking | ____ moth | ____ path |

1. The ____ is in the jug.

2. We can skate at the ice ____.

3. The red pen is in my ____.

4. Can we hike on this ____?

5. Did you ____ for a cookie?

6. A ____ was flying around the lamp.

7. The truck ____ its horn.

8. I saw mother ____ to Beth

Add the suffixes to the words.

1. sweep + ing ____________
2. think + ing ____________
3. skate + ing ____________
4. flap + ing ____________
5. count + ed ____________
6. pluck + ed ____________
7. smile+ ed ____________
8. float + ed ____________

Choose the correct words to finish the sentences. Fill in the circle next to the correct words.

1. Beth was ____________ to her brother.
   - O shout
   - O shouted
   - O shouting

2. The elk ____________ me.
   - O scare
   - O scared
   - O scaring



3. Did you ____________ the plums?
   - O slice
   - O sliced
   - O slicing

4. Hank was ____________ to the sink.
   - O walk
   - O walked
   - O walking

5. Did the soap ____________ in the tub?
   - O float
   - O floated
   - O floating

Read the story.

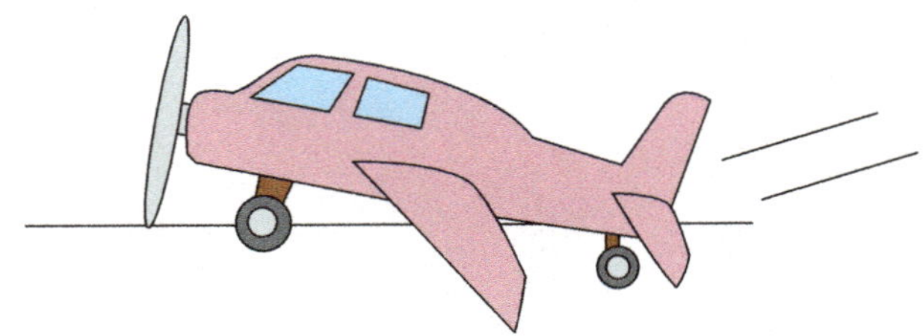

Glen and his father got on a plane. The plane was pink. The plane lifted off. Glen and his father began flying. They flew over a cliff.

The plane glided in the sky. Glen saw a flock of geese. Glen was having fun.

Thump! The plane began to sink. But, Glen was not scared. The tires popped out under the plane.

The plane skidded to a stop. It was a soft landing. Glen's father can fly the plane well.

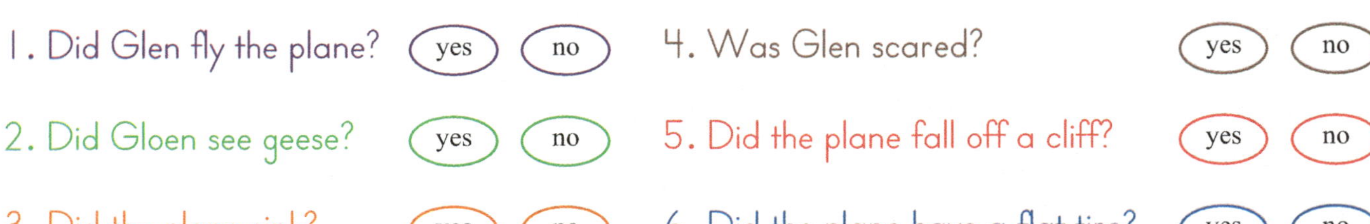

1. Did Glen fly the plane? yes no
2. Did Gloen see geese? yes no
3. Did the plane sink? yes no
4. Was Glen scared? yes no
5. Did the plane fall off a cliff? yes no
6. Did the plane have a flat tire? yes no

Read the sets of words. Find the missing words from the word list in the red box, to tell how the words in the sets are alike. Write the word on the blank line. Not all the words in the list are used.

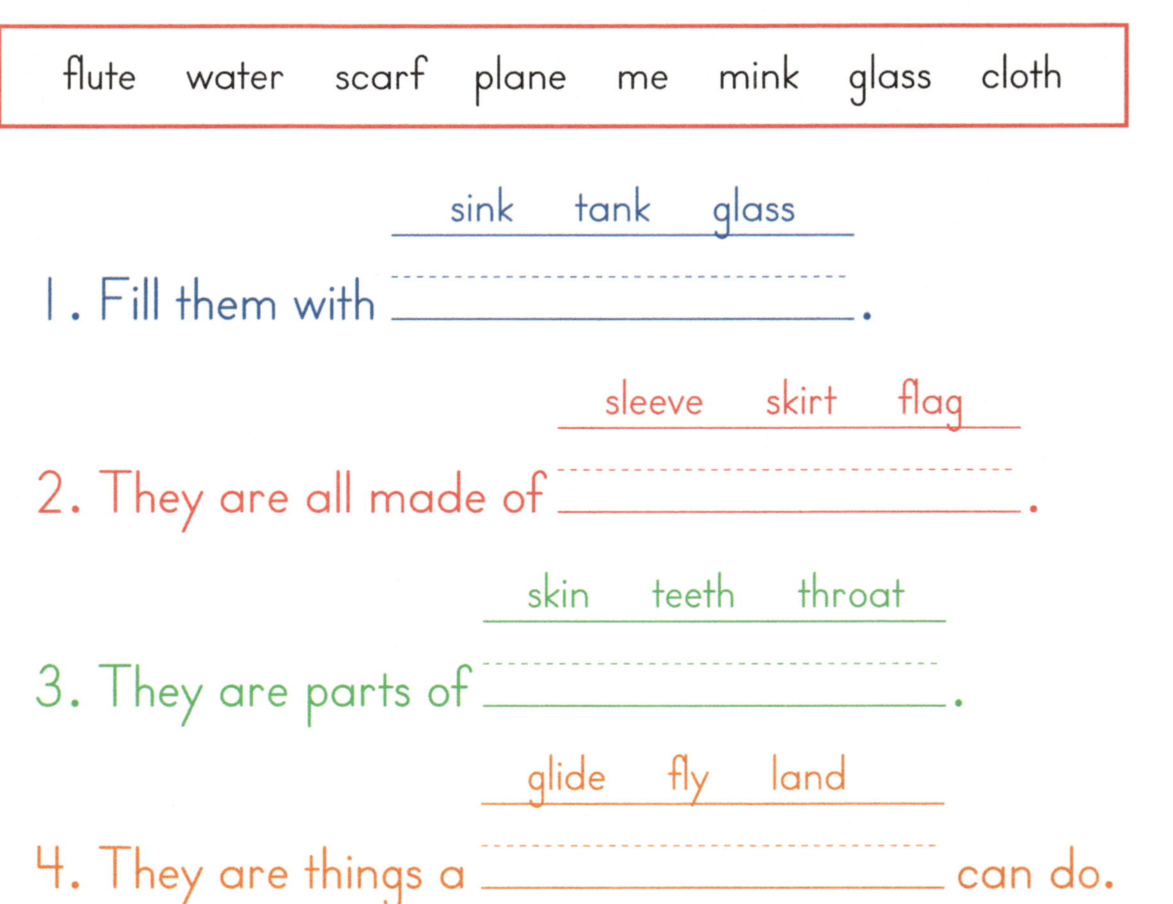

flute water scarf plane me mink glass cloth

sink tank glass

1. Fill them with ______.

sleeve skirt flag

2. They are all made of ______.

skin teeth throat

3. They are parts of ______.

glide fly land

4. They are things a ______ can do.

Add it, her, him, them, or our to the words self or selves to complete the sentences.

| it | her | him | them | our |
|---|---|---|---|---|

The mouse found ____________self in a trap.

He wound up the clock by ____________self .

We found the gold by ____________selves.

They stayed in the house by ____________selves.

She made ____________self a new blouse.

Replace the two words above the lines with a contraction.
Fill in the circle next to the correct way to write the contraction.

We are going to a scout meeting. ○ Wer'e ○ We're ○ We'ar

They are working on the yellow house. ○ The're ○ They'r ○ They're

I am bouncing on the mat. ○ I'am ○ I'm ○ Ia'm

You are walking the hound today. ○ You're ○ Your'e ○ You'ar

It does not have a round snout. ○ doen't ○ doesn't ○ does't

## The Ground That Talked

Use the book to find the sentences.
Fill in the missing word.
Write the page number for the sentence.

"The ground has a ________!" Page ____

A rope is ________ on your snout. Page ____

"I will be glad to," said the ________. Page ____

He was taking me to a dog ________. Page ____

Find the opposites. Match the numbers.

1. himself 2. themselves 3. round 4. out
5. found 6. proud 7. sour 8. theirs

| | | | |
|---|---|---|---|
| ____ lost | ____ in | ____ ashamed | ____ flat |
| ____ sweet | ____ ours | ____ ourselves | ____ herself |

 

Circle the word the teacher says.

| | | | | | |
|---|---|---|---|---|---|
| 1 | ground | grond | grund | gound | groud |
| 2 | sore | shour | shore | sour | sure |
| 3 | shout | scout | scott | scote | scoat |
| 4 | spound | souse | spouse | spond | sound |
| 5 | once | oune | ounce | uonce | oucne |
| 6 | pound | poud | prod | prud | proud |
| 7 | hershelf | herelf | hersef | hersell | herself |
| 8 | abounce | aboun | aboud | abound | aloud |

Fill in the circle next to the word that completes the sentence.

We made cookies by __________?

O ourselves O himself O itself O you're O I'm

The hog's nose is called a __________.

O pig O spout O honker O snout O tilt

The __________ is made of dirt and rocks.

O blouse O ground O around O wound O look

Did the cat __________ on the mouse?

O kiss O hour O pounce O hound O ate

Can you __________ to ten?

O mount O count O noun O mound O pout

106

Read the sentences. Look at the picture to find the missing word. Write the word on the lines. Choose a word in the green box. Not all words will be used.

| button | pepper | rabbit | dinner | kitten | ribbon | mittens | mirror | hammer |
|---|---|---|---|---|---|---|---|---|

The ____________ was stuck in a tree.

The ____________ were in my coat pocket.

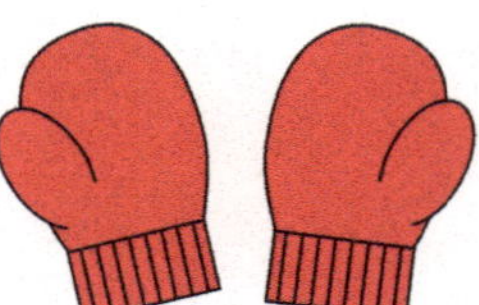

The ____________ and nails were in the box.

The ____________ made me sneeze.

The ____________ hopped into a hole.

Add ing or ed to the words in bold print to complete the sentences correctly.

The stars in the sky **glimmer**__________.

Is father **borrow**__________ a ladder?

I am **button**__________ my shirt.

We **butter**__________ the muffins.

The parrot in the cage was **mutter**__________.

Help the rabbit sort the carrots. Number them in alphabetical order from 1 to 10.

Read the facts about the animals. Fill in the squares at the bottom of the page to show which animal the sentence describes. You will fill in both squares if the sentence is true for both otters and puffins.

**Otters** have brown fur. They have four short legs. They have long tails. Otters have webbed feet. This helps them swim. They eat fish and frogs. Otters like to play. They slide on the snow or mud into lakes.

**Puffins** are birds. They have short wings. Puffins have webbed feet. They are black and white. Sometimes they are also red and yellow. They dig a burrow about three feet deep. They lay one egg in the hole. Puffins swim well. They eat fish.

I have 4 short legs. ☐ Otter ☐ Puffin

I have short wings. ☐ Otter ☐ Puffin

I like to swim. ☐ Otter ☐ Puffin

I eat frogs. ☐ Otter ☐ Puffin

I am a bird. ☐ Otter ☐ Puffin

I like to play. ☐ Otter ☐ Puffin

I am black and white. ☐ Otter ☐ Puffin

I have webbed feet. ☐ Otter ☐ Puffin

I have brown fur. ☐ Otter ☐ Puffin

I have a long tail. ☐ Otter ☐ Puffin

I lay eggs. ☐ Otter ☐ Puffin

I eat fish. ☐ Otter ☐ Puffin

 

Answer the questions about *Super Pork Saves the Kitten.*

**Super Pork Saves the Kitten**

Did Herb hide in a tree?  no

Was the parrot's name Pepper? 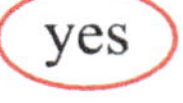 no

Did Super Pork lasso the bull?  no

Was the kitten gray? yes no

Did Super Pork save the dog?  

Use the book to find the sentences. Fill in the missing word. Write the page number for the sentence.

A yellow kitten had __________ in a nest. Page _____

I will name you __________," said Herb. Page _____

Mort __________ his shirt. Page _____

Super Pork made the __________ into a lasso. Page _____

110

Fill in the circle next to the word the teacher says.

| 1 | 2 | 3 | 4 |
|---|---|---|---|
| O batter | O shimmer | O offer | O clatter |
| O better | O shudder | O off | O classic |
| O bitter | O stutter | O office | O clutter |
| O butter | O stagger | O effort | O collar |

| 5 | 6 | 7 | 8 |
|---|---|---|---|
| O mitten | O rubber | O letter | O parrot |
| O muffin | O rudder | O litter | O pepper |
| O mutton | O ribbon | O lesson | O pillar |
| O mutter | O rabbit | O lasso | O platter |

Fill in the circle next to the word that completes the sentence.

We like to put ____________ on toast.

O borrow O butter O cannot O yellow O better

The ____________ played in the river.

O funnel O other O hollow O otter O shudder

I can kick a ____________ ball.

O trigger O sudden O dinner O cottage O soccer

We are ____________ nails.

O hammering O hit O hammer O upper

I saw my face in the ____________.

O roller O mirror O traffic O pillow O puffin

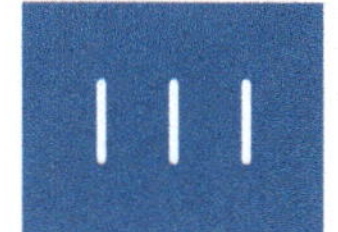


Read the sentences. Look at the picture to find the missing word. Choose a word from the box at the top of the page. Write the word on the lines. Not all words will be used.

| goose | noon | loose | broom | boots | moose | tools | stool | spoon |
|---|---|---|---|---|---|---|---|---|

The ______________ had huge hooves.

The ______________ feel too loose.

We will use ______________ to fix the room.

The ______________ swooped over the lake.

I will sit on a ______________ to eat my food.

## The Cool Moose

There's a moose in my swimming pool
He's just relaxing, looking cool
He thinks that he has found the spot
To take a break when it is hot

I have news for that antlered goon
I'll drain the pool this afternoon
Soon he'll know it's time to scoot
For I'll give that moose the boot

That moose has me in a bad mood
That's why I sit here, why I brood
He squished my ducky I have proof
It's still stuck there on his hoof

Find the words in the poem that have the long *oo* sound as in moon.

Read about the animals.

**Loons** are big birds. They have long bills and look like ducks. Loons can swim under water. They swim well. They eat fish. They can't walk on land. Loons lay two brown eggs. They make nests out of plants. They are black and white.

**Raccoons** have gray fur with black tips. They have a ringed tail. They live in hollow trees or rocks. Raccoons swim well. They eat fish and frogs. Raccoons also eat rats, mice, and grain.

**Coots** are also birds. They are gray and black. They look like ducks. They swim well. They eat plants and snails. They do not have webbed feet. They lay brown eggs.

In the boxes, fill in the L box if it describes a Loon. Fill in the C box if it describes a coot. Fill in the R box if it describes a raccoon. More than one animal may fit the descriptions. More than one box can be filled in.

R = Raccoon  L = Loon  C = Coot

R L C I eat snails.

R L C I eat fish.

R L C My home is a tree.

R L C I can't walk on land.

R L C I am a bird.

R L C I have black on me.

R L C I have a ringed tail.

R L C I lay brown eggs.

R L C I look like a duck.

R L C I swim well.

R L C I have a long bill.

R L C I have fur.

 

114

Answer the questions about *The Moose's Tooth.*

| | | |
|---|---|---|
| Did the moose bite a rock? | yes | no |
| Was the doctor a raccoon? | yes | no |
| Did the doctor pull out a tooth? | yes | no |
| Did the raccoon get a red balloon? | yes | no |
| Was the nurse a goose? | yes | no |

Replace the two words above the lines with a contraction.
Fill in the circle next to the correct way to write the contraction.

| | | | |
|---|---|---|---|
| We will ___ go to the zoo. | O Well | O We'il | O We'll |
| I think you will ___ like the goose | O you'll | O you'wi | O you'ill |
| He will ___ shoot hoops with Dad. | O He'll | O H'ill | O Hew'll |
| I will ___ put the tooth in a jar. | O Iw'll | O I'il | O I'll |
| She will ___ swim in the pool. | O Shell | O She'll | O Shew'll |
| They will ___ feed the baboon. | O The'll | O Theyw'll | O They'll |

Fill in the circle next to the word the teacher says.

| 1 | 2 | 3 | 4 |
|---|---|---|---|
| ○ boot | ○ drop | ○ grove | ○ swoop |
| ○ booth | ○ door | ○ goof | ○ swoon |
| ○ boost | ○ droop | ○ groom | ○ scoop |
| ○ boo | ○ brood | ○ hoove | ○ scoot |
| ○ broom | ○ broop | ○ groove | ○ soop |

| 5 | 6 | 7 | 8 |
|---|---|---|---|
| ○ trap | ○ cartoot | ○ noon | ○ dome |
| ○ troop | ○ cart | ○ moo | ○ dune |
| ○ trip | ○ caboose | ○ moan | ○ doom |
| ○ toop | ○ cartoon | ○ moon | ○ done |
| ○ trooq | ○ tune | ○ moose | ○ mood |

Fill in the circle next to the word that completes the sentence.

The ____________ on the lake was honking.

○ goose ○ soon ○ gloom ○ cool ○ goof

Is your baby tooth ____________?

○ loss ○ boom ○ loop ○ coop ○ loose

I will sweep with that ____________.

○ roof ○ swoon ○ loot ○ gloom ○ broom

Is a hammer a ____________?

○ stoop ○ igloo ○ tool ○ toot ○ loon

You can eat with a ____________.

○ loom ○ spoon ○ coat ○ spool ○ zoom

# 116

Read the sentences. Look at the picture to find the missing word. Choose a word from the box at the top of the page. Write the word on the lines. Not all words will be used.

| chain | chore | chicken | chest | chase | chop | child | much | cheese |
|---|---|---|---|---|---|---|---|---|

The ______________ was sitting on the couch.

The ______________ laid an egg.

We had cheddar ______________ and chips.

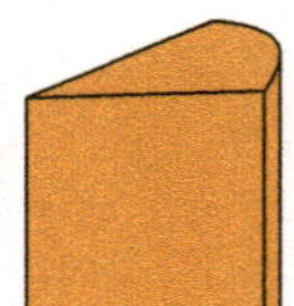

The ______________ is made of steel.

The ______________ was full of gold.

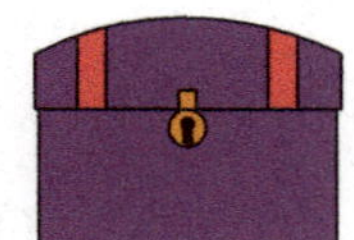

 

Read each group of words. They are alike in some way. Write the number from the word list that completes the descriptions.

1. face 2. names 3. chirp 4. lunch 5. food 6. pouch 7. ranch

_____ chicken, cheese, chips — They are things you can eat at _____.

_____ Chester, Chuck, Mitch — They are _____.

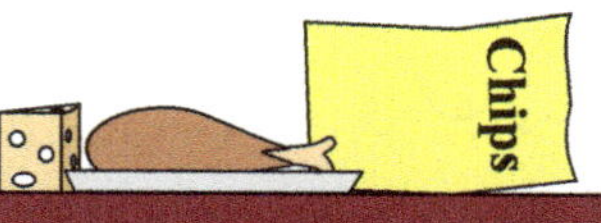


_____ sheep, horses, steers — You can see them at a _____.

_____ cheek, chin, nose — They are parts of your _____.

_____ crunch, munch, chomp — They are ways to bite _____.

The mother and father left the zoo with the chimp. What happened to Chester? Solve the code to find out.

___ ___ ___ ___ ___ ___ ___
3 8 5 19 20 5 18

___ ___ ___
23 1 19

___ ___ ___ ___ ___ ___
8 9 4 9 14 7

___ ___ ___
9 14 1

___ ___ ___ ___ ___ ___ ___ ___ ' ___
11 1 14 7 1 18 15 15 19

___ ___ ___ ___ ___
16 15 21 3 8

| | |
|---|---|
| 1 | A |
| 2 | B |
| 3 | C |
| 4 | D |
| 5 | E |
| 6 | F |
| 7 | G |
| 8 | H |
| 9 | I |
| 10 | J |
| 11 | K |
| 12 | L |
| 13 | M |
| 14 | N |
| 15 | O |
| 16 | P |
| 17 | Q |
| 18 | R |
| 19 | S |
| 20 | T |
| 21 | U |
| 22 | V |
| 23 | W |

118

Read about the chipmunks.

**Chipmunks** are small rodents. They are also called ground squirrels. They are about six inches long. They have stripes on their backs. Often, they'll stuff their cheeks with food.

Chipmunks eat many things. Chipmunks gather nuts, grains, and seeds. in their cheeks. They put food in the pouches. They store food for the winter.

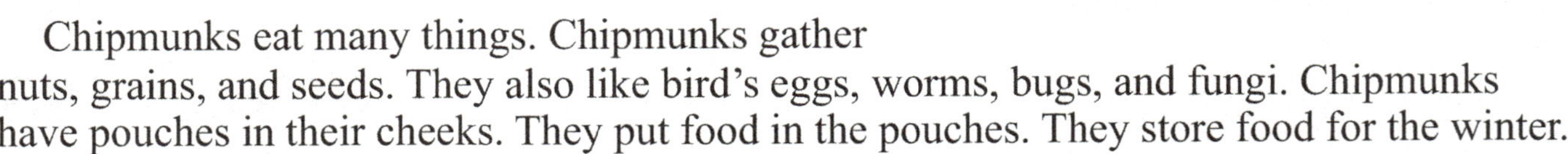

Chipmunks eat many things. Chipmunks gather nuts, grains, and seeds. They also like bird's eggs, worms, bugs, and fungi. Chipmunks have pouches in their cheeks. They put food in the pouches. They store food for the winter.

Chipmunks dig tunnels in the ground. The tunnels can be ten feet long. They make nests in the tunnel. The chipmunks keep their nests clean.

They look very cute. You may want to pick one up. Don't try. They may become afraid and bite. A bite can make you sick.

Read the descriptions. Is the description true about chipmunks? If so, fill in the yes oval. If it is not true, fill in the no circle.

1. I eat bird's eggs. yes no
2. I am a rodent. yes no
3. I live in trees. yes no
4. I can dig in the ground. yes no
5. I have stripes on my back. yes no
6. I like to be picked up. yes no
7. I have a pouch in my cheek. yes no
8. I am ten inches long. yes no
9. I keep my nest clean. yes no
10. I make tunnels a mile long. yes no

 

Answer the questions about *Chester at the Zoo*.

Was the baby named Chuck?  yes  no

Did the chimp eat eggs? yes  no

Did the baby find French fries? yes 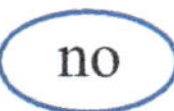 no

Was Doctor French a vet? yes  no

Did a bird take the chips?  yes  no

## Chester at the Zoo

**Sentence Hunt**

Use the book to find the sentences. Fill in the missing word. Write the page number for the sentence.

Chester began to ________ the chips. Page ____

Chester was behind the ________. Page ____

They had a ________ of cheese. Page ____

"I am a doctor for ________," Page ____

 

120

Fill in the circle next to the word the teacher says.

| 1 | 2 | 3 | 4 |
|---|---|---|---|
| ○ notch | ○ ground | ○ finch | ○ charred |
| ○ not | ○ graon | ○ flints | ○ charge |
| ○ natch | ○ grouch | ○ faints | ○ chart |
| ○ noth | ○ grow | ○ flinch | ○ chat |

| 5 | 6 | 7 | 8 |
|---|---|---|---|
| ○ chin | ○ drink | ○ mitch | ○ crutch |
| ○ chum | ○ birch | ○ match | ○ church |
| ○ china | ○ ditch | ○ march | ○ chunk |
| ○ chime | ○ batch | ○ much | ○ crunch |

Fill in the circle next to the word that completes the sentence.

The ____________ ate the chips.

○ children ○ hatch ○ such ○ cheer ○ match

A kangaroo has a ____________.

○ snatch ○ stitch ○ pitch ○ chirp ○ pouch

The horses were on the ____________.

○ hitch ○ hatch ○ munch ○ ranch ○ couch

The ice ____________ into the water.

○ changing ○ changed ○ chance ○ chart ○ change

We ____________ the chimps play.

○ chosen ○ thatch ○ torch ○ watched ○ arch

 

Add a letter to the words in bold print to complete the sentences. Choose a letter from the 3 choices at the end of the sentence. Write the letter on the line.

The bird had a yellow ____________**eak.** p l b

I like to eat ice ____________**ream.** d c f

Did you ____________**ear** the horn honking? y f h

Can I eat the ____________**each**? p r t

The fire made a lot of ____________**eat.** h s m

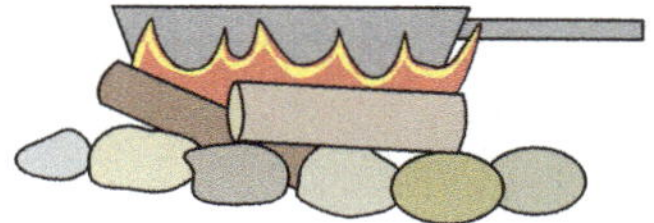

I spilled the drink on my ____________**eans.** d l j

The cut on my hand will ____________**eal.** s p h

Do not ____________**ease** the cat. l t c

Can you ____________**ead** the letters? r l b

There are sharks in the ____________**ea.** t s p

# 122

Trace the dotted lines to break the word into two syllables. Read the words.

tea|cher sea|son sea|horse bea|ver

pea|nuts rea|son ap|pears

Use the words from above to complete the sentences. Write the words on the blanks

The ____________ I like best is summer.

A ____________ can bite trees.

The goose ____________ to be sick.

The ____________ were still in shells.

The ____________ swam in the sea.

The ____________ called my mother.

The dog was barking for no ____________.

 

Read the sentences. Look at the words in the rectangles. Match the numbers by the opposite words to the sentences. Not all the opposites will be used.

1. mean 2. heat 3. disappear 4. rear 5. least 6. cleaned 7. leave

_____ I messed up my room.

_____ We need to cool the food.

_____ The big dog is not nice.

_____ They will come to my house.

_____ I like green beans the most.

Answer the questions about *Emily and the Babysitter.*

yes no Did Elaine really disappear?

yes no Did Elaine clean the dishes?

yes no Was the babysitter named Anna?

yes no Did Elaine say, "Please forgive me"?

yes no Did Emily put peanut butter on her face?

Emily and the Babysitter

Read about peanuts.

**Peanuts** grow under the ground. The peanut is not really a nut. It is more like a pea. The peanuts are seeds. They grow in shells called pods. Peanuts are also called goobers or goober peas.

Peanuts make nice snacks. Many peanuts are used to make peanut butter. The peanuts are roasted. The skins are taken off. The peanuts are then ground up. Other things are added. Salt and sweet things are added.

Peanuts can also be used in making other things. Paint, soap, shaving cream, cheese, and ice cream can be made from peanuts.

Some people get sick from eating peanuts. Keep foods with peanuts away from them. Be aware of friends who cannot eat peanuts. Ask an adult how to keep friends safe if they have a peanut **allergy**.

Read and answer the questions about peanuts.

Do peanuts grow above ground? yes no

Are peanuts also called goober peas? yes no

Can paint be made from peanuts? yes no

Do peanuts make bad snacks? yes no

Is peanut butter made from goober peas? yes no

Besides peanut butter, what foods can be made from peanuts?

1. ________ 2. ________ ________

Peanut shells are called ________.

 

Fill in the circle next to the word the teacher says.

| 1 | 2 | 3 | 4 |
|---|---|---|---|
| ○ bed | ○ leash | ○ seas | ○ clean |
| ○ bad | ○ least | ○ reason | ○ cream |
| ○ dead | ○ lease | ○ season | ○ crease |
| ○ bead | ○ sheet | ○ seahorse | ○ creak |

| 5 | 6 | 7 | 8 |
|---|---|---|---|
| ○ peas | ○ weak | ○ feast | ○ beach |
| ○ peace | ○ leave | ○ feeds | ○ bleach |
| ○ please | ○ wove | ○ east | ○ each |
| ○ peals | ○ weave | ○ feats | ○ breathe |

Fill in the circle next to the word that completes the sentence.

The bird has a short __________.

○ zeal ○ bleak ○ peak ○ beak ○ beast

I have some new blue __________.

○ jeans ○ real ○ tease ○ weave ○ deal

We play on a baseball __________.

○ seam ○ bean ○ east ○ neat ○ team

The pipe began to __________.

○ teach ○ leak ○ peal ○ speak ○ smear

We will rake the __________.

○ lead ○ steal ○ leaves ○ meal ○ mean

 

126

Read the sentences. Look at the picture to find the missing word. Choose a word from the box at the top of the page. Write the word on the lines. Not all words will be used.

| candy | forty | money | daddy | puppy | kitty | bunny | monkey |
|---|---|---|---|---|---|---|---|

The ____________ ate the crunchy leaves.

The ____________ acts silly.

Sally gave me the ____________.

We saw a funny ____________ at the zoo.

The ____________ was happy.

 

Listen to the teacher for directions.

____ hurry ____ carry ____ many ____ fluffy ____ chilly

Read the sentences. Look at the words in the rectangles. Find the word in the list that is the opposite of the word in the rectangle. Match the numbers by the words to the sentences.

____ The kitty was chubby.

____ The sky was dark.

____ The donkey looked sad.

____ My room was clean.

____ The honey tasted icky.

1. yummy
2. mommy
3. happy
4. silly
5. sunny
6. messy
7. skinny

Read the sentences. Look at the words in the rectangles.
Find the number next to the synonym for that word. The list is in red.
Write the number on the lines. Not all words will be used.

_____ The puppy was fuzzy.

_____ The breeze made it feel nippy.

_____ My belly wants food.

_____ The road felt lumpy.

_____ The old man was jolly.

1. tummy
2. every
3. furry
4. sandy
5. chilly
6. happy
7. bumpy

Answer the questions about *Super Pork and the Fuzzy Monster.*

| | | |
|---|---|---|
| Did the fuzzy monster hurt Super Pork? | yes | no |
| Did Spunky play with Kathy? | yes | no |
| Did Mort eat too much candy? | yes | no |
| Did Spunky have a cape? | yes | no |
| Did Super Pork help a bunny? | yes | no |

**Super Pork and the Fuzzy Monster**

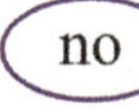


 

Read about turkeys.

**Turkeys** are big birds.
Daddy turkeys are called Toms.
Mommy turkeys are called hens.
Roast turkey is used for food.
Some turkeys are raised on farms.
Other turkeys live in the wild.

Wild turkeys live in small flocks. They fly well. But, they can fly just fly a short way. Turkeys sleep in trees. This is called roosting.

They eat grain, seeds, and bugs. Turkeys like to live near water. Some wild turkeys have red heads. Others have blue heads with red bumps.

Turkeys raised on farms are bigger. Some are white. Some are dark. They lay 25 to 40 eggs each year. Turkeys need to live in clean places. If not, they get sick.

Read and answer the questions about turkeys.

Do some turkeys sleep in trees? yes no

Are mommy turkeys called gobblers? yes no

Do turkeys eat grain? yes no

Are some turkeys green? yes no

Are farm turkeys bigger than wild turkeys? yes no

When a turkey sleeps, it's called ______________________

Turkeys may have two colors of heads:

1. ______________ 2. ______________

130

Fill in the circle next to the word the teacher says.

| 1 | 2 | 3 | 4 |
|---|---|---|---|
| O skippy | O turley | O sixty | O lampy |
| O simpy | O turk | O sickly | O lumpy |
| O skinny | O turkey | O sixteen | O limpy |
| O skimpy | O kurty | O city | O lompy |

| 5 | 6 | 7 | 8 |
|---|---|---|---|
| O diry | O jelly | O every | O kitten |
| O dirty | O holly | O very | O cat |
| O dity | O jolly | O next | O catty |
| O darty | O July | O ever | O kitty |

Fill in the circle next to the word that completes the sentence.

The ____________ swung on a branch.

O monkey O hockey O nippy O money O copy

The beach was ____________.

O hobby O daddy O pushy O sandy O many

My nose was ____________.

O ninety O stuffy O family O army O body

The horse pulled a ____________.

O story O honey O buggy O weedy O fifty

The ____________ was a lot of fun.

O hurry O handy O penny O picky O party

 

Read the story. Circle all the words that have *ou* or *ow*.

Thick clouds were over the lake. "It is going to rain," said the mouse. He began to run to his own house. But, he was too slow. The rain began pounding the mouse.

He hopped into a bowl. Water began to flow from the hill. The bowl flipped over. The mouse held on. It became a boat. The mouse was swept into the lake.

I stopped raining. But, the mouse was too far out in the lake. A crow flew over. "Will you give me a tow?" asked the mouse.

"Yes," said the crow. "I will throw you a string."

The crow flew off and found a spool of string. The crow came back in about an hour. The mouse wound the string around the bowl. The crow towed the mouse home.

Read and answer the questions about the story. Fill in the answer to the sentences yes or no.

| | | |
|---|---|---|
| Did a trout tow the mouse? | yes | no |
| Did the mouse hop in the bowl? | yes | no |
| Did the crow find a string? | yes | no |
| Was it snowing? | yes | no |
| Was the mouse running to his hound? | yes | no |

Choose the correct words to finish the sentences. Fill in the circles next to the correct words.

The rabbit was a ___________.

- O cannon O otter O puppet

Can I borrow a ___________.

- O pillow O matter O current

I will ___________ the nail.

- O hammer O lasso O offer

This ___________ tastes better.

- O sputter O cottage O butter

The kitten has a yellow ___________.

- O shimmer O collar O stutter

Read the sets of words. Three of the words are alike in some way. One word is different. Circle the different word.

1. house church cottage switch
2. sunny beach rainy cloudy
3. collar button spoon pocket
4. puppy chicken goose turkey
5. tooth ear pretty chin

 

Choose the correct words to finish the sentences. Fill in the circles next to the correct words.

The donkey on the couch was ____________.

O sleepy O valley O many

I like ____________ butter and jelly.

O fluffy O cream O peanut

The hungry puppy was ____________.

O picky O skinny O bumpy

Honey is so ____________.

O furry O sticky O tummy

Did Randy eat the ____________ bar?

O candy O wacky O thirty

Read the words. Match the opposites. Write the numbers on the lines.

| | | | |
|---|---|---|---|
| 1. house | 2. weak | 3. catch | 4. slow |
| 5. messy | 6. runny | 7. gloomy | 8. lumpy |

_____ neat _____ throw _____ cherry _____ lost _____ fast

133

Choose the correct words to finish the sentences. Fill in the circles next to the correct words.

We are

leaving the beach.

He will

feed the turkey.

They are

inside the house.

She will

read a story.

They will

bounce the yellow ball.

Read the words. Match the synonyms. Write the numbers on the lines.

| | | | |
|---|---|---|---|
| 1. dirty | 2. sandy | 3. catch | 4. throw |
| 5. happy | 6. neat | 7. father | 8. tummy |

____ pitch ____ daddy ____ messy ____ belly ____ gritty

 

Read the sentences. Look at the picture to find the missing word. Choose a word from the box at the top of the page. Write the word on the lines. Not all words will be used.

| rattle | cattle | bottle | wobble | table | noodle | turtle | jungle | apples |
|---|---|---|---|---|---|---|---|---|

The ________________ is made of glass.

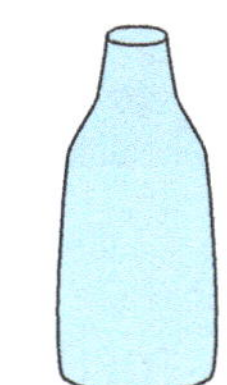

________________ grow on trees.

We saw a ________________ at the creek.

The baby can shake the ________________.

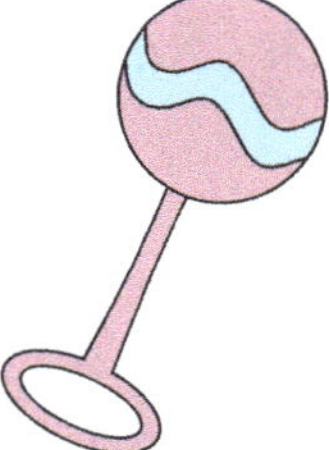

A bumble bee is on the ________________.

Read about turtles.

*Red Eared Sliders*

**Turtles** have shells and no teeth. Some turtles live on land. Other turtles live in the water. Turtles live a long time. Some turtles live 150 years. Turtles grow to many sizes. The small turtles are about 3 inches long. Some turtles can grow up to nine feet long.

A turtle's shell has two parts. The upper part is shaped like a dome. The lower part is flat. The turtle's bones are part of the shape. Turtles lay eggs on land. Some turtles lay up to 200 eggs. Turtles put dirt or sand over the eggs. The mother turtle then leaves the eggs.

Some turtles eat meat. Others eat plants. Some eat both. Turtles eat a lot at one time. Then, they may not eat for weeks.

*Loggerhead Sea Turtle hatchling*

*Alligator Snapping Turtle*

Read and answer the questions about turtles.

Do turtle shells have three parts? yes no

Do turtles have teeth? yes no

Do turtles lay eggs on land? yes no

Are some turtles nine feet long? yes no

Do turtles eat plants? yes no

Some turtles live ______________ years.

The upper shell of a turtle is shaped like a ______________.

 

Answer the questions about *The Turtle and the Bunny.*

Did Twiddle run faster than Bubbles? yes no

Did Bubbles get a turtle bike? yes no

Did Bubbles make the turtles dizzy? yes no

Did the bike cost thirty bundles of carrots? yes no

Did Twiddle put on goggles? yes no

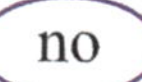

The Turtle and the Bunny

Use the book to find the sentences. Fill in the missing word. Write the page number for the sentence.

"I can pedal a bike faster than a __________." Page ______

Mr. Doodle was in the __________. Page ______

"It's better to be __________." Page ______

It will cost you fifty __________ of carrots." Page ______

140

Fill in the circle next to the word the teacher says.

| 1 | 2 | 3 | 4 |
|---|---|---|---|
| O settle | O hassle | O picle | O qibble |
| O sittle | O halse | O pikle | O quibble |
| O shuttle | O hasle | O pichle | O quible |
| O shutle | O hale | O pickle | O quobble |

| 5 | 6 | 7 | 8 |
|---|---|---|---|
| O fabble | O wigle | O doodle | O sipple |
| O fabele | O wiggle | O dodle | O supply |
| O fable | O wiggly | O doddle | O sample |
| O sable | O wiggy | O dooddle | O simple |

Fill in the circle next to the word that completes the sentence.

Milk is in the ___________.

O grapple O tattle O thistle O cobble O bottle

We put the ___________ on the horse.

O jumble O stubble O saddle O middle O little

Is the dog a ___________?

O poodle O bundle O table O missle O brittle

Did the man ___________ the roses for a nickel?

O kettle O turtle O dimple O peddle O cable

Was that a ___________ bee?

O cuddle O fumble O giggle O bumble O rubble

 

Read the sentences. Look at the picture to find the missing word. Choose a word from the box at the top of the page. Write the word on the lines. Not all words will be used.

| door | rook | hook | would | look | book | floor | cookie | foot |
|---|---|---|---|---|---|---|---|---|

I took the funny ________.

I have a wool sock on my ________.

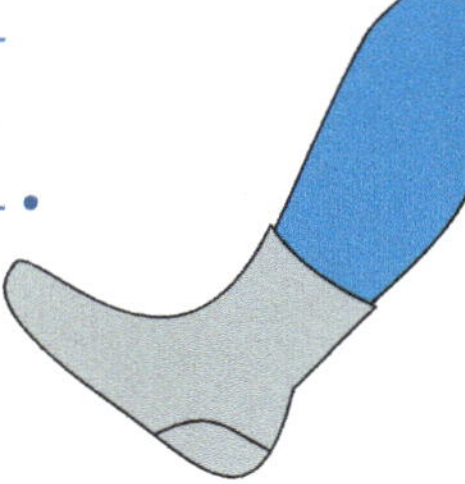

The ________ is made of wood.

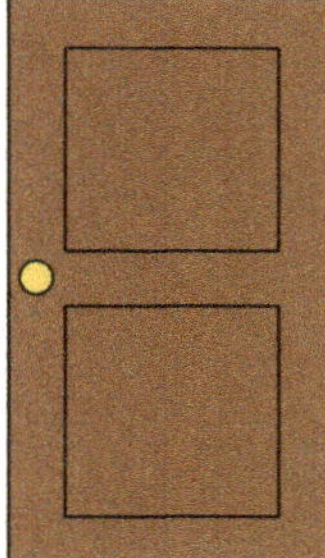

The ________ was very good.

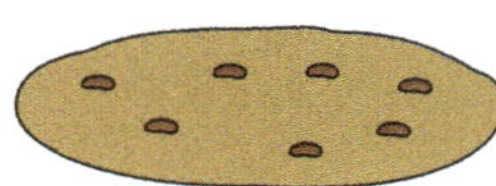

I tossed a ________ into the brook.

142

Read the sentences clues. Choose a word from the box that matches the clue. Write the number on the lines.

| | | | | |
|---|---|---|---|---|
| 1. floor | 2. good | 3. hook | 4. door | 5. wood |
| 6. cook | 7. foot | 8. woof | 9. roof | 10. book |

_____ Open this to get into a room.

_____ Put a sock on it.

_____ It's full of words.

_____ You stand on this in a house.

_____ It should keep out the rain.

_____ This is something a dog could say.

_____ You do this to food.

_____ If you are not bad, you are

_____ Trees are made of this.

_____ A fish could bit this.

Read the sentences. Fill in a word to make each sentence true. Look at the boxes before each sentence. If the letter **C** is in the box, write **could** or **couldn't** on the line.
If the letter **S** is in the box, write **should** or **shouldn't** on the line.
If the letter **W** is in the box, write **would** or **wouldn't** on the line.

C You ____________ eat cookies.

W You ____________ see with your foot.

S You ____________ be a crook.

C You ____________ grow wool on your nose.

S A horse ____________ have a hoof.

Read the sentences. A word is underlined. Before each sentence is a box.
Put the letter **V** in the box if it is a **verb**. Put the letter **N** in the box if it is a **noun**.

☐ 1. The cook made us lunch.

☐ 2. Will you cook us lunch?

☐ 3. I can hook a fish.

☐ 4. I will hang my coat on the hook.

☐ 5. I took the foot stool.

☐ 6. Would you close the door?

☐ 7. We will look at the roof.

Answer the questions about *It Could Have Been, Would Have Been, Jonathan.*

**It Could Have Been, Would Have Been, Jonathan**

Did Jonathan have a birthday party? yes no

Was a rubber snake in Rosie's purse? yes no

Did boats float on the floor? yes no

Did Grandpa blow bubbles? yes no

Did Teddy hide in a swimming pool? yes no

Read about wool.

**Wool** comes from sheep. Wool can come from goats and rabbits, too. Wool is used to make rugs, blankets, and clothes.

Most wool is white. It can also be tan, brown, or black. Cutting off the wool is called shearing. As it is cut, the wool comes off as one part. The wool cut from the sheep is called a fleece.

The wool is cleaned. It can then be dyed to be all kinds of colors. It can then be spun. This makes it into yarn. The yarn can be used to make cloth.

Read and answer the questions about wool.

1. Can wool come from rabbits? yes no
2. Can wool come from pigs? yes no
3. Is some wool tan? yes no
4. Is yarn made of wool? yes no
5. Is cutting off the wool called shearing? yes no

Wool cut from sheep is called ____________________.

Wool can make __________, __________, and __________.

 

Fill in the circle next to the word the teacher says.

| 1 | 2 | 3 | 4 |
|---|---|---|---|
| ○ four | ○ wild | ○ cook | ○ poore |
| ○ floor | ○ wode | ○ crook | ○ por |
| ○ frool | ○ would | ○ krooc | ○ poor |
| ○ foor | ○ wooldhale | ○ crok | ○ pure |

| 5 | 6 | 7 | 8 |
|---|---|---|---|
| ○ noodle | ○ woof | ○ shook | ○ book |
| ○ noke | ○ woff | ○ sook | ○ broke |
| ○ koon | ○ wool | ○ stook | ○ brake |
| ○ nook | ○ woofy | ○ skoosh | ○ brook |

Fill in the circles next to the words that answer the questions.

What is something sweet to eat?

○ nook ○ hood ○ could ○ cookie

What is a part of a house?

○ good ○ roof ○ soot ○ rook

What comes from trees?

○ wood ○ cook ○ would ○ poor

What is the same as a creek?

○ book ○ crook ○ brook ○ should

What is sheep fur called?

○ could ○ hook ○ wool ○ woof

146

Read the sentences. Look at the picture to find the missing word. Choose a word from the box at the top of the page. Write the word on the lines. Not all words will be used.

| knock | light | comb | knife | wrestle | thumb | wrench | right | lamb | write |
|---|---|---|---|---|---|---|---|---|---|

I will use a ________________ on the tight bolt.

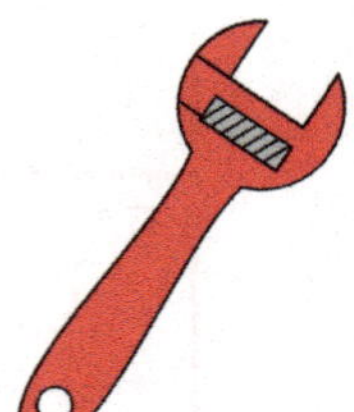

The ________________ might cut the knot.

The ________________ climbed up the hill.

The ________________ was very bright.

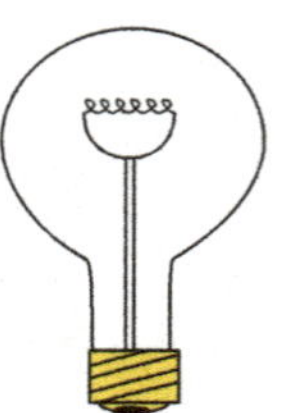

The knuckle on my ________________ got cut.

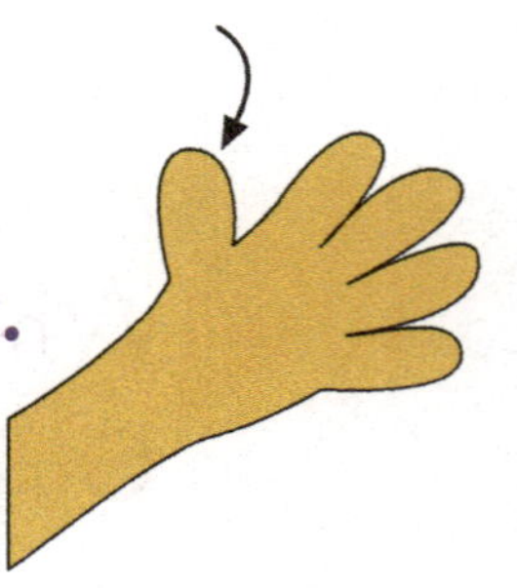

 

Write the number next to the word that sounds alike.

1. need 2. ring 3. rap 4. Neal 5. sight

____ wrap ____ kneel ____ site ____ wring ____ knead

Fill in the circles next to the words that answer the questions.

The apples are too ____ to reach.

O hi O high

Can you ____ a letter?

O right O write

Do you ____ how to add?

O no O know

It is dark at ____.

O night O knight

There is a ____ in the rope.

O knot O not

 

Read about knights.

**Knights** were called sir. Training began at the age of 7 or 8. The child would go and live with a lord. A **lord** was like a king. The child was called a **page**. There was a lot of things for pages to learn. Pages had to know how to ride horses. They had to know how to hunt.

But they also learned to read and write. They learned math. The page learned about God. They played games. They played chess and checkers on cold days.

A knight's job was to fight for the lord. At the age of 20 the man became a knight. The lord gave the man a light tap on the neck. The lord would say, "In the name of God, I dub thee a knight."

Read and answer the questions about knights.

| | | |
|---|---|---|
| Did knights learn to dance? | yes | no |
| Did a knight become a page? | yes | no |
| Did a lord fight for the knights? | yes | no |
| Did knights know how to read? | yes | no |
| Did a page live with his mom and dad? | yes | no |

A man became a knight at the age of ________________.

Knights sometimes played ____________ and ____________.

 

Answer the questions about *I'm Not Lyin'*.

Did a roar frighten Rosie?  

Did Grandpa get a flat tire?  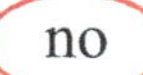

Did Momma step on a nail?  

Was the lion named June?  

Did cattle play on the swing?  

Use the book to find the sentences. Fill in the missing word. Write the page number for the sentence.

The pan was ______________ off the stove. Page ______

Rosie took her ______________ to me. Page ______

"Who ______________ the garage?" Page ______

"The ______________ roast is gone," said Momma. Page ______

150

Fill in the circle next to the word the teacher says.

| 1 | 2 | 3 | 4 |
|---|---|---|---|
| ○ wrinkle | ○ knackle | ○ nigt | ○ tumb |
| ○ wriggle | ○ knickle | ○ night | ○ thumb |
| ○ rink | ○ kneckle | ○ niht | ○ tomb |
| ○ wrinke | ○ knuckle | ○ nigh | ○ thum |

| 5 | 6 | 7 | 8 |
|---|---|---|---|
| ○ weave | ○ comb | ○ kneel | ○ high |
| ○ reave | ○ chrome | ○ knel | ○ tight |
| ○ wreath | ○ crumb | ○ knell | ○ hight |
| ○ writhe | ○ cumb | ○ keel | ○ thigh |

Fill in the circles next to the words that answer the questions.

Who might need a wrench to fix a pipe?

○ doctor ○ king ○ plumber ○ writer

What is at the end of an arm?

○ bomb ○ knee ○ right ○ wrist

Who was a page?

○ knight ○ fight ○ lamb ○ wren

What means not dark?

○ knit ○ bright ○ numb ○ wriggle

What can cut?

○ climb ○ knife ○ wrath ○ slight

 

Read the sentences. Look at the picture to find the missing word. Choose a word from the box at the top of the page. Write the word on the lines. Not all words will be used.

| flowers | howl | cow | crowd | tower | wow | crown | drowse | owl | drown |
|---|---|---|---|---|---|---|---|---|---|

The ______________ ate the hay.

The ______________ smelled nice.

The queen had a gold ______________.

The ______________ was watching a mouse.

The ______________ was very high.

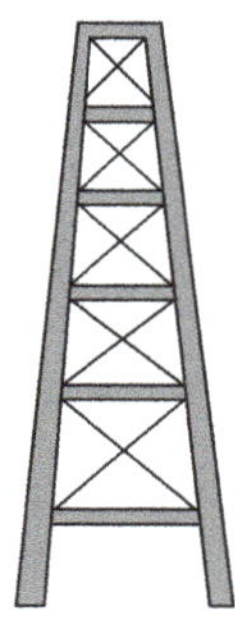

## Cow Town

I once went to a real cow town
And hoofed it up in a beef hoedown
The cow band played along all night
Those fiddling cows were quite the sight.

The band was dressed in red and blue
They sang their songs with a drawn out moo
When they were done they took a bow
And invited me to eat some chow

All along I mixed right in
Until I made a Cow Town sin
They gave me corn that was really sweet
I said,"No thanks, I'll just have meat"

A hush fell over the bovine crowd
I said a word that wasn't allowed
So if you can help please send me mail
Address it to the Cow Town Jail

Find the *ow* words. Write them on the lines.

 

Read about owls.

*Northern Spotted Owl*

**Owls** have round faces. They have hooked beaks. Owls may be brown or gray. Some have specks. Owls hunt at night. Owls must turn their heads to see. They can turn their heads all the way around. This lets them see behind their backs.

Owls eat mice and rats. Large owls may also eat skunks, rabbits, and ducks. Owls have good ears. They can hear things to hunt. Owls eat in trees. They eat all of the animal. Later they spit up the fur and bones. You can find pellets by an owl's tree. These are the fur and bones from their food.

*Great Horned Owl chicks with downy*

Owls make homes in hollow trees or in rocks. They make poor nests. They lay one to seven eggs. The eggs hatch after 4 to 5 weeks. The chicks have downy feathers. These feathers do not help them fly. Downy keeps the chicks from getting cold. Later, they grow flight feathers. At three months old, owls begin to fly.

*Saw-whet Owl*

Read and answer the questions about owls.

Do owls have round faces?
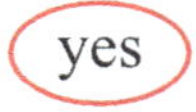

Do owls make good nests?

Can three month old owls fly?

Write five things owls can eat.

Answer the questions about *Farmer Brown's Cow.*

Did the plumber sell a cow?  

Did Farmer Green own the cow? yes 

Did the cow dive into a pool? yes 

Was a man going to eat Flower? yes 

Did Flower bite a man? yes 

**Farmer Brown's Cow**

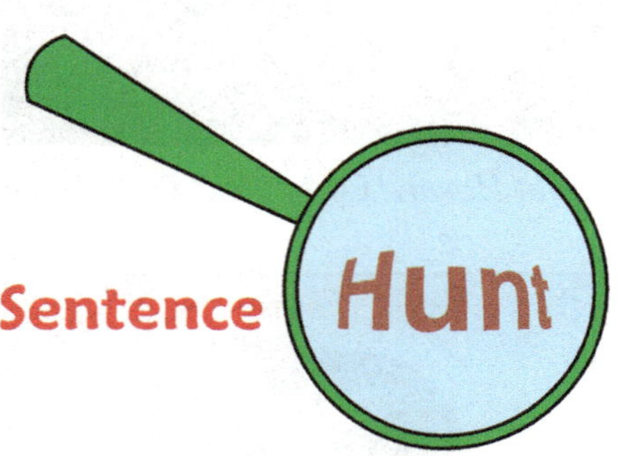


Use the book to find the sentences. Fill in the missing word. Write the page number for the sentence.

The ______________ was all around her. Page ______

She liked ______________ around. Page ______

His truck broke ______________. Page ______

That made Farmer Brown ______________. Page ______

 

Fill in the circle next to the word the teacher says.

| 1 | 2 | 3 | 4 |
|---|---|---|---|
| O bowse | O scowl | O down | O wow |
| O brow | O showl | O drowl | O vow |
| O drowse | O sowl | O drown | O wov |
| O browse | O cowls | O bown | O vowel |

| 5 | 6 | 7 | 8 |
|---|---|---|---|
| O kowd | O joyl | O cower | O fown |
| O crows | O jaw | O crower | O frown |
| O crowd | O jown | O crowner | O fawn |
| O cowd | O jowl | O cowed | O frower |

Fill in the circles next to the words that answer the questions.

What is very high?

O sow O scowl O tower O drown

What will a wolf do at the moon?

O howl O prowl O power O wow

What did kings have?

O bow O crown O how O clown

What eats grass?

O plow O drowse O gown O cow

What might a dog do?

O down O growl O fowl O pow

# 156

Read the sentences. Look at the picture to find the missing word. Choose a word from the box at the top of the page. Write the word on the lines. Not all words will be used.

| splashed | splat | squirrel | string | screen | shrank | shrimp |
|---|---|---|---|---|---|---|

The ______________ scrambled up the tree.

I think my new shirt ______________.

The fish ______________ in the stream.

A red ______________ is on the yo-yo.

The plate was full of ______________.

Read the sentences. If the underlined word is a **verb**, write **V** on the lines before the sentence. If it is a **noun**, write **N** on the lines.

N = noun V = verb

_____ The zebra has black stripes.

_____ I scraped my knee.

_____ A squid has lots of arms.

_____ Could we splice the two ropes?

_____ Did you shred the cheese?

_____ The spring broke in the couch.

Look at the pairs of words. If they are **synonyms**, write **S** on the lines. If they are **antonyms**, write an **A** on the lines.

S = synonym A = antonym, opposite

_____ shrink grow

_____ scream yell

_____ street road

_____ spray dry

_____ scribble doodle

_____ strong weak

_____ squeak growl

_____ shrub bush

 

Read about squirrels.

**Squirrels** have long tails. The word squirrel means "shade tailed". Squirrels like to jump. As they fly, their tails help them steer.

Squirrels have sharp teeth. They can cut into a shell of a nut. Squirrels also eat seeds, grain, and bird's eggs.

There are many kinds of tree squirrels. There are gray squirrels, red squirrels, black squirrels, and flying squirrels. Their sharp claws help them grip tree bark.

Flying squirrels do not really fly. They glide from tree to tree. They have a flap of skin. The skin is between the front and back legs. Most flying squirrels are ten inches long. Some flying squirrels are three feet long.

Read and answer the questions about squirrels.

Do squirrels eat eggs? yes no

Are there blue squirrels? yes no

Can squirrels cut into nut shells? yes no

Are some squirrels four feet long? yes no

Do squirrels steer with their tails? yes no

What does the word squirrel mean? ______________________.

What helps flying squirrels glide? a ____________ of ____________.

 

Answer the questions about *Squeaky Shrinks*.

**Squeaky Shrinks**

Was Scruffy a squirrel?  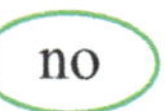


Did Squeaky scrape his knee? yes 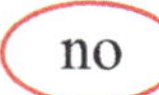


Did Squeaky think he shrunk? yes 

Did Scruffy strum a banjo? yes 

Did Squeaky really shrink? yes 

Use the book to find the sentences. Fill in the missing word. Write the page number for the sentence.

"Did you ______ your wrist? Page ______

The rock struck the ______ mud. Page ______

Then, Squeaky began to ______. Page ______

"We have to ______ you," Page ______

# 160

Fill in the circle next to the word the teacher says.

| 1 | 2 | 3 | 4 |
|---|---|---|---|
| O scrippy | O shed | O splurge | O spain |
| O skippy | O said | O spurge | O sprain |
| O scap | O shred | O surge | O spane |
| O scrappy | O stred | O slurge | O sprian |

| 5 | 6 | 7 | 8 |
|---|---|---|---|
| O squorn | O srabble | O shrunch | O struggle |
| O squarm | O saddle | O scrunch | O straggle |
| O squirm | O strabble | O strunch | O striggle |
| O sqirm | O straddle | O sprunch | O stroggle |

Fill in the circles next to the words that answer the questions.

What is a place to fish?

O stress O shrug O sprinkle O stream

What means to make bigger?

O squint O stretch O splat O scrimp

What lives in a tree?

O stride O sprig O squirrel O scroll

What means to clean something?

O scrub O shrill O split O strut

What means to become smaller?

O splice O spree O shrink O squire

# 161

Read the sentences. Look at the picture to find the missing word. Choose a word from the box at the top of the page. Write the word on the lines. Not all words will be used.

| join | coin | point | crowd | toy | soy | oil | voice | moist | choice | soil |
|---|---|---|---|---|---|---|---|---|---|---|

We put the flower in good ________________.

We played with the ________________ trucks.

I will count my ________________.

The rain made the ground ________________.

Stop!

Ray shouted with a loud ________________.

162

Read the sets of words. Match the descriptions to the words. Write the numbers.

1. boil, broil 2. soil, rocks 3. coins, dollars 4. boy, girl
5. Roy, Joyce 6. voice, noise 7. hogs, pigs

____ They are part of the ground.

____ They are kinds of money.

____ They are kinds of children.

____ They are ways to cook.

____ They are sounds.

____ They say oink.

____ They are names.

Read the sentences. If the underlined word is a **verb**, write **V** on the lines before the sentence. If it is a **noun**, write **N** on the lines.

N = noun V = verb

____ Did you boil the food?

____ We wrapped the meat in foil.

____ She will oil the squeaky bike.

____ He will plant the seeds in moist soil.

 

Answer the questions about Roy's Old Coin.

## Roy's Old Coin

| | | |
|---|---|---|
| Was a can in the soil? | yes | no |
| Would the snake make lots of noise? | yes | no |
| Did Joyce need ten dollars? | yes | no |
| Did Joyce sell a coin? | yes | no |
| Was the can an oil can? | yes | no |

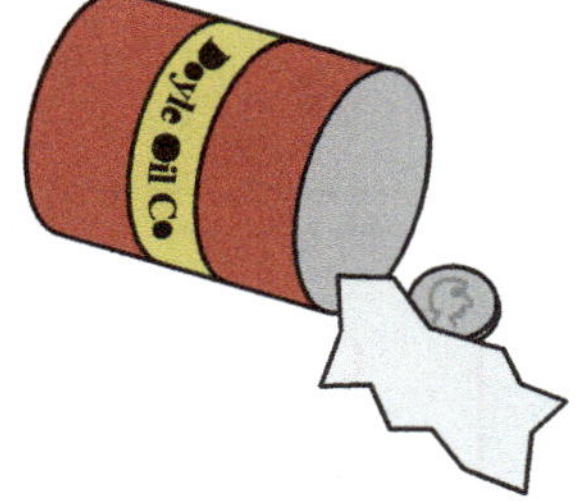

Use the book to find the sentences. Fill in the missing word.
Write the page number for the sentence.

"I want to sell my ______," said Roy. Page ______

He heard a clank ______. Page ______

"It might have a ______. Page ______

"I don't want the food to ______." Page ______

165

Fill in the circle next to the word the teacher says.

| 1 | 2 | 3 | 4 |
|---|---|---|---|
| ○ poy<br>○ loy<br>○ ploy<br>○ proy | ○ poise<br>○ poick<br>○ poyz<br>○ ploise | ○ voice<br>○ void<br>○ voil<br>○ voy | ○ Joy<br>○ Joys<br>○ Joich<br>○ Joyce |

| 5 | 6 | 7 | 8 |
|---|---|---|---|
| ○ spoil<br>○ soil<br>○ sproil<br>○ ploil | ○ boil<br>○ broil<br>○ sloil<br>○ broint | ○ coy<br>○ shoy<br>○ soy<br>○ stoy | ○ choose<br>○ choice<br>○ choich<br>○ coich |

Fill in the circles next to the words that answer the questions.

What can you spend?

○ point ○ coy ○ foil ○ coin

What makes a sound?

○ noise ○ royal ○ ploy ○ toil

What is something to play with?

○ hoist ○ moist ○ toy ○ soy

What is like a happy feeling?

○ void ○ joy ○ oil ○ spoil

What did a pig say?

○ poise ○ boy ○ oink ○ voice

Read the sentences. Look at the picture to find the missing word. Choose a word from the box at the top of the page. Write the word on the lines. Not all words will be used.

| hawk | crawl | dawn | draw | fawn | raw | saw | trawl | straw | paw |
|---|---|---|---|---|---|---|---|---|---|

We can drink the malt with a ____________________.

The ____________________ has big claws.

We used the ____________________ to cut the wood.

A ____________________ ran across the lawn.

The hound hurt his ____________________.

167

Read the sentences. Choose words from the box at the top of the page.
Fill in the blank with the number of the word that tells about the sentence.

| 1. awful | 2. saw | 3. bawl | 4. crawl | 5. hawk |
|---|---|---|---|---|
| 6. straw | 7. fawn | 8. dawn | 9. law | 10. yawn |

_____ The first part of the day.

_____ This is a big bird.

_____ You drink with this.

_____ Open your jaw to do this.

_____ This means to cry hard.

_____ If something is very badly.

_____ A baby and a bug can do this.

_____ This can cut things.

_____ Follow this or go to jail.

_____ A baby deer.

 

Read about hawks.

**Hawks** are found all over the world. They are like eagles. They have strong claws. The claws can grab their food.

Hawks hunt in the day time. Some farmers think hawks kill hens. Most hawks do not hurt farm animals. They eat rats, mice, rabbits, and other birds. Their hooked beaks cut their food apart.

Hawks make nests of sticks. They make nests on cliffs, hills, and trees. Their eggs are white or light blue. Most have brown spots. Baby hawks have white down. Down is fuzzy. A baby hawk can fly after about six weeks.

Read and answer the questions about hawks.

Do hawks make nests of straw? yes no

Can baby hawks fly after six weeks? yes no

Do most hawks hunt at night? yes no

Do most hawks eat hens? yes no

Are hawks like eagles? yes no

What are four things a hawk might eat?

What do hawk eggs look like?

Answer the questions about *The Hawk That Bawled.*

| | | |
|---|---|---|
| Did the hawk eat a mouse? | yes | no |
| Did the birds bawl? | yes | no |
| Did the hawk eat a bug? | yes | no |
| Did the birds say the hawk was not fair? | yes | no |
| Did the rabbit have a flaw? | yes | no |

The Hawk That Bawled

Use the book to find the sentences. Fill in the missing word. Write the page number for the sentence.

"A ____________ is too big," bawled the hawk. Page ______

The ____________ bounced free on the lawn. Page ______

"I had a mouse in my ____________. Page ______

"Rabbits have a ____________," Page ______

 

Fill in the circle next to the word the teacher says.

| 1 | 2 | 3 | 4 |
|---|---|---|---|
| O squarl | O lawn | O flaw | O gawn |
| O scawrl | O law | O faw | O gawk |
| O scawl | O wall | O fraw | O jawk |
| O scrawl | O low | O flawn | O gawl |

| 5 | 6 | 7 | 8 |
|---|---|---|---|
| O tall | O paw | O braw | O awe |
| O trawn | O pawl | O bawn | O awk |
| O trawl | O pawn | O brawn | O awn |
| O trawk | O pown | O brain | O yaw |

Fill in the circles next to the words that answer the questions.

What might you do if you're tired?

O draw O caw O yawn O gawk

What is something a baby can do?

O slaw O crawl O awful O squaw

What are hawk's feet?

O shawls O fawns O paws O claws

What means bad?

O awful O raw O drawn O law

What can you use to drink?

O haw O bawl O dawn O straw

171

Read the sentences. Choose the missing word from the box.
Write the number in the blank next to each sentence. Not all words will be used.

| 1. bumble | 2. puddle | 3. apple | 4. wiggle | 5. rattle | 6. struggle | 7. riddle | 8. jungle |
|---|---|---|---|---|---|---|---|

____ The baby squealed when it found the ________.

____ The monkey's home is in the ________.

____ The ________ bee crawled on the table.

____ It will be a ________ to lift the box.

____ The turtle nibbled on the ________.

Read the sentence clues. Write the number of the sentence clue on the lines before the words.

1. This is at the end of your leg.
2. This has pages.
3. What can you do to food?
4. What is a horse's foot called?
5. This comes from trees.
6. What could a dog say?
7. This person steals things.
8. What is sheep fur called?
9. This is a part of a car.
10. This tastes good.

____ woof ____ cookie ____ crook ____ foot ____ hood

____ cook ____ wool ____ hoof ____ book ____ wood

 

Read the words and match them to their antonyms (opposites). Write the numbers on the lines.

1. big    2. awful    3. chomp    4. gave    5. sat

____ stood    ____ little    ____ nibble    ____ good    ____ took

Choose a description that tells how the two words are alike.
Write the number next to the description.

| | |
|---|---|
| 1. saw, knife | ____ baby animals |
| 2. hoof, paw | ____ ways to cook eggs |
| 3. fiddle, banjo | ____ joints in our bones |
| 4. dime, penny | ____ things to strum |
| 5. lamb, fawn | ____ use a pen to do this |
| 6. wrist, knee | ____ things that cut |
| 7. jungle, lawn | ____ things that swim |
| 8. draw, write | ____ animal feet |
| 9. scramble, boil | ____ kinds of coins |
| 10. shrimp, squid | ____ places plants grow |

# 172

Read the sentences. Add the silent letters to the words in bold print.

1. I bumped my ___**nee** last **ni**___ ___**t.**
2. The **plum**___**er** had a ___**rench.**
3. I ___**now** how to ___**rite.**
4. The ___**nife** cut my **thum**___.
5. Did I **com**___ my hair **ri**___ ___**t**?

Read the sentences. Choose the missing word from the box.
Write the number in the blank next to each sentence. Not all words will be used.

| 1. clown | 2. tower | 3. cow | 4. gown | 5. growl | 6. pow | 7. flower | 8. crowded |
|---|---|---|---|---|---|---|---|

___ The ________ slept on the straw.

___ Can I pick the yellow ________?

___ The ________ had a big red nose.

___ The ________ is very high.

___ The town was ________.

___ The mean dog began to ________.

___ She had a pink ________.

 

Read the sentences. Choose the missing word from the two choices at the end of the sentence. Write the word in the blank.

1. This is ________ cow. (hour, our)

2. The sun will rise at ________. (dawn, don)

3. The cookies were too ________ to reach. (hi, high)

4. Did she ________ the gift? (rap, wrap)

5. Is the boy named ________? (Kneel, Neal)

Match the synonyms. Write the numbers on the lines.

1. kettle 2. wreck 3. road 4. shrub 5. squirt 6. rip 7. squeeze

____ squish ____ bush ____ pot

____ street ____ shred ____ spray ____ smash

 